Careers in Focus

BROADCASTING

THIRD EDITION

Ferguson

An imprint of Infobase Publishing

Careers in Focus: Broadcasting, Third Edition

Copyright © 2007 by Infobase Publishing

Ferguson
An imprint of Infobase Publishing
132 West 31st Street
New York NY 10001

ISBN-10: 0-8160-6567-5
ISBN-13: 978-0-8160-6567-7

Library of Congress Cataloging-in-Publication Data

Careers in focus. Broadcasting.—3rd ed.
    p. cm.
  Includes index.
  ISBN 0-8160-6567-5 (hc : alk. paper)
  1. Broadcasting—Vocational guidance—Juvenile literature. I. Title: Broadcasting.
  HE8689.4.C37 2007
  384.54023'73--dc22   2006033428

Text design by David Strelecky
Cover design by Salvatore Luongo

Printed in the United States of America

MP MSRF 10 9 8 7 6 5 4 3 2 1

This book is printed on acid-free paper.

Table of Contents

Introduction

Broadcasting is the electronic transmission of images and/or sound. Radio and television are the main broadcasting media. The radio and television industry is made up of a large number of relatively small and independent stations that are individually owned and operated. Approximately 327,000 people are employed in both radio and TV. Commercial radio employs about half and commercial television about one-third of the total. Others are employed by broadcasting headquarters, including network offices and public broadcasting stations.

Broadcasting is particularly exciting because it is like show business with a stopwatch; programming is timed down to the second, and precision and speed are crucial for both taped and live broadcasts. Broadcasting relies on the creativity of its employees to develop and hold the interest of its listening and viewing audiences. Yet, because of the unremitting pressures of deadlines, broadcasting must be geared to quick decisions and quick action.

Opportunities are available for those interested in pursuing performance-related careers (actors, announcers, disc jockeys, reporters, sports broadcasters, and weather forecasters), those interested in working behind the scenes in creative positions (animators, art directors, directors, editors, and producers), and those interested in technical support positions (broadcast engineers and lighting technicians). There are also opportunities in talent management, real-time captioning, and radio and television station management.

Earnings in broadcasting range from less than $13,000 for beginning disc jockeys and announcers to more than $1 million for top actors, directors, and other professionals in the field.

Careers in government are available to those with a wide variety of educational backgrounds. For example, entry-level positions such as production assistants require only a high school diploma. Other broadcasting careers require some postsecondary training (announcer, broadcast engineer, disc jockey, lighting technician) or a bachelor's degree (art director, media planner, media buyer, program director, real-time captioner, and television director). Some careers, such as actor and animator, require creative talent rather than formal education.

Employment in the radio and television broadcasting industry is expected to increase about as fast as the average—about 11 percent—for all other industries through 2014, according to the U.S.

Department of Labor. Competition is the name of the game in the broadcasting industry. The public has many viewing and listening choices, from cable, satellite TV, and conventional television to radio and Web broadcasts. This bodes well for workers as the industry expands and competes for listeners and viewers. However, job seekers should be prepared for stiff competition, since this field is an attractive and popular career choice. Be prepared to work in a smaller market to gain experience; most large market stations, such as Chicago and New York, prefer to hire experienced workers.

Each article in this book discusses a particular broadcasting career in detail. The articles in *Careers in Focus: Broadcasting* appear in Ferguson's *Encyclopedia of Careers and Vocational Guidance* but have been updated and revised with the latest information from the U.S. Department of Labor, professional organizations, and other sources. The following paragraphs detail the sections and features that appear in the book.

The **Quick Facts** section provides a brief summary of the career, including recommended school subjects, personal skills, work environment, minimum educational requirements, salary ranges, certification or licensing requirements, and employment outlook. This section also provides acronyms and identification numbers for the following government classification indexes: the Dictionary of Occupational Titles (DOT), the Guide to Occupational Exploration (GOE), the National Occupational Classification (NOC) Index, and the Occupational Information Network (O*NET)-Standard Occupational Classification System (SOC) index. The DOT, GOE, and O*NET-SOC indexes have been created by the U.S. government; the NOC index is Canada's career classification system. Readers can use the identification numbers listed in the Quick Facts section to access further information about a career. Print editions of the DOT (*Dictionary of Occupational Titles*. Indianapolis, Ind.: JIST Works, 1991) and GOE (*The Complete Guide for Occupational Exploration*. Indianapolis, Ind.: JIST Works, 1993) are available at libraries. Electronic versions of the NOC (http://www23.hrdc-drhc.gc.ca) and O*NET-SOC (http://online.onetcenter.org) are available on the Internet. When no DOT, GOE, NOC, or O*NET-SOC numbers are present, this means that the U.S. Department of Labor or Human Resources Development Canada has not created a numerical designation for this career. In this instance, you will see the acronym "N/A" or not available.

The **Overview** section is a brief introductory description of the duties and responsibilities involved in this career. Oftentimes, a career may have a variety of job titles. When this is the case, alternative career titles are presented. The **History** section describes the history of the particular job as it relates to the overall development of its industry or field. The **Job** describes the primary and secondary duties of the job. **Requirements** discusses high school and postsecondary education and training requirements, any necessary certification or licensing, and other personal requirements for success in the job. **Exploring** offers suggestions on how to gain experience in or knowledge of the particular job before making a firm educational and financial commitment. The focus is on what can be done while still in high school (or in the early years of college) to gain a better understanding of the job. The **Employers** section gives an overview of typical places of employment for the job. **Starting Out** discusses the best ways to land that first job, be it through the college placement office, newspaper ads, or personal contact. The **Advancement** section describes what kind of career path to expect from the job and how to get there. **Earnings** lists salary ranges and describes the typical fringe benefits. The **Work Environment** section describes the typical surroundings and conditions of employment—whether indoors or outdoors, noisy or quiet, social or independent. Also discussed are typical hours worked, any seasonal fluctuations, and the stresses and strains of the job. The **Outlook** section summarizes the job in terms of the general economy and industry projections. For the most part, Outlook information is obtained from the U.S. Bureau of Labor Statistics and is supplemented by information taken from professional associations. Job-growth terms follow those used in the *Occupational Outlook Handbook*. Growth described as "much faster than the average" means an increase of 27 percent or more. Growth described as "faster than the average" means an increase of 18 to 26 percent. Growth described as "about as fast as the average" means an increase of 9 to 17 percent. Growth described as "more slowly than the average" means an increase of 0 to 8 percent. "Decline" means a decrease by any amount. Each article ends with **For More Information,** which lists organizations that provide information on training, education, internships, scholarships, and job placement.

    Careers in Focus: Broadcasting also includes photos, informative sidebars, and interviews with professionals in the field.

Actors

OVERVIEW

Actors play parts or roles in dramatic productions on the stage, in motion pictures, or on television or radio. They impersonate, or portray, characters by speech, gesture, song, and dance. There are approximately 62,600 actors working in the United States.

HISTORY

Drama, which began as a component of religious festivals, was refined as an art form by the ancient Greeks, who used the stage as a forum for topical themes and stories. The role of actors became more important than in the past, and settings became more realistic with the use of scenery. Playgoing was often a great celebration, a tradition carried on by the Romans. The rise of the Christian church put an end to theater in the sixth century AD, and for several centuries actors were ostracized from society, surviving as jugglers and jesters.

Drama was reintroduced during the Middle Ages but became more religious in focus. Plays during this period typically centered on biblical themes, and roles were played by craftspeople and other amateurs. This changed with the rediscovery of Greek and Roman plays in the Renaissance. Professional actors and acting troupes toured the countries of Europe, presenting ancient plays or improvising new dramas based on cultural issues and situations of the day. Actors began to take on more prominence in society. In England, actors such as Will Kemp and Richard Burbage became known for their roles in the plays of William Shakespeare. In France, Molière wrote and often acted in his own plays.

QUICK FACTS

School Subjects
English
Theater/dance

Personal Skills
Artistic
Communication/ideas

Work Environment
Indoors and outdoors
Primarily multiple locations

Minimum Education Level
High school diploma

Salary Range
$14,290 to $25,022 to $116,168+

Certification or Licensing
None available

Outlook
About as fast as the average

DOT
150

GOE
01.03.02

NOC
5135

O*NET-SOC
27-2011.00

Until the mid-17th century, however, women were banned from the stage, and the roles of women were played by young boys.

By the 18th century, actors could become quite prominent members of society, and plays were often written—or, in the case of Shakespeare's plays, rewritten—to suit a particular actor. Acting styles tended to be highly exaggerated, with elaborate gestures and artificial speech, until David Garrick introduced a more natural style to the stage in the mid-1700s. The first American acting company was established in Williamsburg, Virginia, in 1752, led by Lewis Hallan. In the next century, many actors became stars: Famous actors of the time included Edwin Forrest, Fanny and Charles Kemble, Edmund Kean, William Charles Macready, and Joseph Jefferson, who was particularly well known for his comedic roles.

Until the late 19th century, stars dominated the stage. But in 1874, George II, Duke of Saxe-Meiningen, formed a theater troupe in which every actor was given equal prominence. This ensemble style influenced others, such as Andre Antoine of France, and gave rise to a new trend in theater called naturalism, which featured far more realistic characters in more realistic settings than before. This style of theater came to dominate the 20th century. It also called for new methods of acting. Konstantin Stanislavsky of the Moscow Art Theater, who developed an especially influential acting style that was later called method acting, influenced the Group Theater in the United States; one member, Lee Strasberg, founded the Actors Studio in New York, which would become an important training ground for many of the great American actors. In the early 20th century, vaudeville and burlesque shows were extremely popular and became the training ground for some of the great comic actors of the century.

By then, developments such as film, radio, and television offered many more acting opportunities than ever before. Many actors honed their skills on the stage and then entered one of these new media, where they could become known throughout the nation and often throughout the world. Both radio and television offered still more acting opportunities in advertisements. The development of sound in film caused many popular actors from the silent era to fade from view, while giving rise to many others. But almost from the beginning, film stars were known for their outrageous salaries and lavish style of living.

In the United States, New York gradually became the center of theater and remains so, although community theater companies abound throughout the country. Hollywood is the recognized center of the motion picture and television industries. Other major production centers are Miami, Chicago, San Francisco, and Austin.

THE JOB

The imitation or basic development of a character for presentation to an audience often seems like a glamorous and fairly easy job. In reality, it is demanding, tiring work that requires special talent.

The actor must first find a part available in some upcoming production. This may be in a comedy, drama, musical, or opera. Then, having read and studied the part, the actor must audition before the director and other people who have control of the production. This requirement is often waived for established artists. In film and television, actors must also complete screen tests, which are scenes recorded on film, at times performed with other actors, which are later viewed by the director and producer of the film.

If selected for the part, the actor must spend hundreds of hours in rehearsal and must memorize many lines and cues. This is especially true in live theater; in film and television, actors may spend less time in rehearsal and sometimes improvise their lines before the camera, often performing several attempts, or "takes," before the director is satisfied. Television actors often take advantage of teleprompters, which scroll their lines on a screen in front of them while performing. Radio actors generally read from a script, and therefore rehearsal times are usually shorter.

In addition to such mechanical duties, the actor must determine the essence of the character being portrayed and the relation of that character to the overall scheme of the play. Radio actors must be especially skilled in expressing character and emotion through voice alone. In many film and theater roles, actors must also sing and dance and spend additional time rehearsing songs and perfecting the choreography. Some roles require actors to perform various stunts, which can be quite dangerous. Most often, these stunts are performed by specially trained *stunt performers*. Others work as *stand-ins* or *body doubles*. These actors are chosen for specific features and appear on film in place of the lead actor; this is often the case in films requiring nude or seminude scenes. Many television programs, such as game shows, also feature *models*, who generally assist the host of the program.

Actors in the theater may perform the same part many times a week for weeks, months, and sometimes years. This allows them to develop the role, but it can also become tedious. Actors in films may spend several weeks involved in a production, which often takes place on location (that is, in different parts of the world). Television actors involved in a series, such as a soap opera or a situation comedy, also may play the same role for years, generally in 13-week cycles. For these actors, however, their lines change from week to week and even from day to day, and much time is spent rehearsing their new lines.

While studying and perfecting their craft, many actors work as *extras*, the nonspeaking characters who appear in the background on screen or stage. Many actors also continue their training. A great deal of an actor's time is spent attending auditions.

REQUIREMENTS

High School
There are no minimum educational requirements to become an actor. However, at least a high school diploma is recommended.

Postsecondary Training
As acting becomes more and more involved with the various facets of our society, a college degree will become more important to those who hope to have an acting career. It is assumed that the actor who has completed a liberal arts program is more capable of understanding the wide variety of roles available. Therefore, it is strongly recommended that aspiring actors complete at least a bachelor's degree program in theater or the dramatic arts. In addition, graduate degrees in the fine arts or in drama are nearly always required should the individual decide to teach dramatic arts.

College can also serve to provide acting experience for the hopeful actor. More than 500 colleges and universities throughout the country offer dramatic arts programs and present theatrical performances. Actors and directors recommend that those interested in acting gain as much experience as possible through acting in plays in high school and college or in those offered by community groups. Training beyond college is recommended, especially for actors interested in entering the theater. Joining acting workshops, such as the Actors Studio, can often be highly competitive.

Other Requirements
Prospective actors will be required not only to have a great talent for acting but also a great determination to succeed in the theater and motion pictures. They must be able to memorize hundreds of lines and should have a good speaking voice. The ability to sing and dance is important for increasing the opportunities of the young

actor. Almost all actors, even the biggest stars, are required to audition for a part before they receive the role. In film and television, they will generally complete screen tests to see how they will appear on film. In all fields of acting, a love for acting is a must. It might take many years for an actor to achieve any success, if at all.

Performers on the Broadway stages must be members of the Actors' Equity Association before being cast. While union membership may not always be required, many actors find it advantageous to belong to a union that covers their particular field of performing arts. These organizations include the Actors' Equity Association (stage), Screen Actors Guild (motion pictures and television films), and American Federation of Television and Radio Artists (TV, recording, and radio). In addition, some actors may benefit from membership in the American Guild of Variety Artists (nightclubs, and so on), American Guild of Musical Artists (opera and ballet), or organizations such as the Hebrew Actors Union or Guild of Italian American Actors for productions in those languages.

EXPLORING

The best way to explore this career is to participate in school or local theater productions. Even working on a props or lighting crew will provide insight into the field.

Also, attend as many dramatic productions as possible and try to talk with people who either are currently in the theater or have been at one time. They can offer advice to individuals interested in a career in the theater.

Many books, such as *Beginning* (New York: St. Martin's Press, 1989), by Kenneth Branagh, have been written about acting, not only concerning how to perform but also about the nature of the work and its offerings, advantages, and disadvantages.

EMPLOYERS

Motion pictures, television, and the stage are the largest fields of employment for actors, with television commercials representing as much as 60 percent of all acting jobs. Most of the opportunities for employment in these fields are either in Los Angeles or New York. On stage, even the road shows often have their beginning in New York, with the selection of actors conducted there along with rehearsals. However, nearly every city and most communities present local and regional theater productions.

As cable television networks continue to produce more and more of their own programs and films, they will become a major provider of employment for actors. Home video will also continue to create new acting jobs, as will the music video business.

The lowest numbers of actors are employed for stage work. In addition to Broadway shows and regional theater, there are employment opportunities for stage actors in summer stock, at resorts, and on cruise ships.

STARTING OUT

Probably the best way to enter acting is to start with high school, local, or college productions and to gain as much experience as possible at that level. Very rarely is an inexperienced actor given an opportunity to perform on stage or in film in New York or Hollywood. The field is extremely difficult to enter; the more experience and ability beginners have, however, the greater their possibilities for entrance.

Those venturing to New York or Hollywood are encouraged first to have enough money to support themselves during the long waiting and searching period normally required before a job is found. Most will list themselves with a casting agency that will help them find a part as an extra or a bit player, either in theater or film. These agencies keep names on file along with photographs and a description of the individual's features and experience, and if a part comes along that may be suitable, they contact that person. Very often, however, names are added to their lists only when the number of people in a particular physical category is low. For instance, the agency may not have enough athletic young women on their roster, and if the applicant happens to fit this description, her name will be added.

ADVANCEMENT

New actors will normally start in bit parts and will have only a few lines to speak, if any. The normal procession of advancement would then lead to larger supporting roles and then, in the case of theater, possibly to a role as understudy for one of the main actors. The understudy usually has an opportunity to fill in should the main actor be unable to give a performance. Many film and television actors get their start in commercials or by appearing in government and commercially sponsored public service announcements, films, and programs. Other actors join the afternoon soap operas and continue on to evening programs. Many actors have also gotten their

Actor–comedian Chris Rock discusses his television series *Everybody Hates Chris* during an interview. *(Landov)*

start in on-camera roles such as presenting the weather segment of a local news program. Once an actor has gained experience, he or she may go on to play stronger supporting roles or even leading roles in stage, television, or film productions. From there, an actor may go on to stardom. Only a very small number of actors ever reach that pinnacle, however.

Some actors eventually go into other, related occupations and become drama coaches, drama teachers, producers, stage directors, motion picture directors, television directors, radio directors, stage managers, casting directors, or artist and repertoire managers. Others may combine one or more of these functions while continuing their career as an actor.

EARNINGS

The wage scale for actors is largely controlled through bargaining agreements reached by various unions in negotiations with producers. These agreements normally control the minimum salaries, hours of work permitted per week, and other conditions of employment. In addition, each artist enters a separate contract that may provide for higher salaries.

In 2007, the minimum daily salary of any member of the Screen Actors Guild (SAG) in a speaking role was $759 or $2,634 for a five-day workweek. Motion picture actors may also receive additional payments known as residuals as part of their guaranteed salary. Many motion picture actors receive residuals whenever films, TV shows, and TV commercials in which they appear are rerun, sold for TV exhibition, or put on videocassette. Residuals often exceed the actors' original salary and account for about one-third of all actors' income.

A wide range of earnings can be seen when reviewing the Actors' Equity Association's *Annual Report,* which includes a breakdown of average weekly salaries by contract type and location. According to the report, for example, those in "Off Broadway" productions earned an average weekly salary of $724 during the 2004-05 season. Other average weekly earnings for the same period include: San Francisco Bay area theater, $307; New England area theater, $314; DisneyWorld in Orlando, Fla., $723; and Chicago area theater, $517. The report concludes that the median weekly salary for all contract areas is $541. Most actors do not work 52 weeks per year; in fact, the report notes that Equity members in good standing only worked an average 16.7 weeks during the 2004–05 season, with median earnings of $6,675.

According to the U.S. Department of Labor, the median yearly earnings of all actors was $25,022 in 2004. The department also reported the lowest-paid 10 percent earned less than $14,290 annually, while the highest-paid 10 percent made more than $116,168.

The annual earnings of persons in television and movies are affected by frequent periods of unemployment. Unions offer health, welfare, and pension funds for members working over a set number of weeks a year. Some actors are eligible for paid vacation and sick time, depending on the work contract.

In all fields, well-known actors have salary rates above the minimums, and the salaries of the few top stars are many times higher. Actors in television series may earn tens of thousands of dollars per week, while a few may earn as much as $1 million or more per week. Salaries for these actors vary considerably and are negotiated individually. In film, top stars may earn as much as $20 million per film, and, after receiving a percentage of the gross earned by the film, these stars can earn far, far more.

Until recent years, female film stars tended to earn lower salaries than their male counterparts; the emergence of stars such as Julia Roberts, Jodie Foster, Halle Berry, and others has started to reverse that trend. The average annual earnings for all motion picture actors, however, are usually low for all but the best-known performers because of the periods of unemployment.

WORK ENVIRONMENT

Actors work under varying conditions. Those employed in motion pictures may work in air-conditioned studios one week and be on location in a hot desert the next.

Those in stage productions perform under all types of conditions. The number of hours employed per day or week vary, as do the number of weeks employed per year. Stage actors normally perform eight shows per week with any additional performances paid for as overtime. The basic workweek after the show opens is about 36 hours unless major changes in the play are needed. The number of hours worked per week is considerably more before the opening, because of rehearsals. Evening work is a natural part of a stage actor's life. Rehearsals often are held at night and over holidays and weekends. If the play goes on the road, much traveling will be involved.

A number of actors cannot receive unemployment compensation when they are waiting for their next part, primarily because they have not worked enough to meet the minimum eligibility requirements for compensation. Sick leaves and paid vacations are not usually available to the actor. However, union actors who earn the minimum qualifications now receive full medical and health insurance under all the actors' unions. Those who earn health plan benefits for 10 years become eligible for a pension upon retirement. The acting field is very uncertain. Aspirants never know whether they will be able to get into the profession, and, once in, there are uncertainties as to whether the show will be well received and, if not, whether the actors' talent can survive a bad show.

OUTLOOK

Employment in acting is expected to grow about as fast as average through 2014, according to the U.S. Department of Labor. There are a number of reasons for this. The growth of satellite and cable television in the past decade has created a demand for more actors, especially as the cable networks produce more and more of their own programs and films. The rise of home video has also created new acting jobs, as more and more films are made strictly for the home video market. Many resorts built in the 1980s and 1990s present their own theatrical productions, providing more job opportunities for actors. Jobs in theater, however, face pressure as the cost of mounting a production rises and as many nonprofit and smaller theaters lose their funding.

Despite the growth in opportunities, there are many more actors than there are roles, and this is likely to remain true for years to come. This is true in all areas of the arts, including radio, television, motion pictures, and theater, and even those who are employed are normally employed during only a small portion of the year. Many actors must supplement their income by working as secretaries, waiters, taxi drivers, and so on. Almost all performers are members of more than one union in order to take advantage of various opportunities as they become available.

It should be recognized that of the 62,600 or so actors in the United States today, only a small percentage are working as actors at any one time. Of these, few are able to support themselves on their earnings from acting, and fewer still will ever achieve stardom. Most actors work for many years before becoming known, and most of these do not rise above supporting roles. The vast majority of actors, meanwhile, are still looking for the right break. There are many more applicants in all areas than there are positions. As with most careers in the arts, people enter this career out of a love and desire for acting.

FOR MORE INFORMATION

The following is a professional union for actors in theater and "live" industrial productions, stage managers, some directors, and choreographers.

Actors' Equity Association
165 West 46th Street
New York, NY 10036-2501
Tel: 212-869-8530
Email: info@actorsequity.org
http://www.actorsequity.org

This union represents television and radio performers, including actors, announcers, dancers, disc jockeys, newspersons, singers, specialty acts, sportscasters, and stuntpersons.

American Federation of Television and Radio Artists
260 Madison Avenue
New York, NY 10016-2401
Tel: 212-532-0800

Email: aftrany@aftra.com
http://www.aftra.com

A directory of theatrical programs may be purchased from NAST.
For answers to a number of frequently asked questions concerning
education, visit the NAST's Web site.
National Association of Schools of Theatre (NAST)
11250 Roger Bacon Drive, Suite 21
Reston, VA 20190-5248
Tel: 703-437-0700
Email: info@arts-accredit.org
http://www.nast.arts-accredit.org

The following union provides general information on actors, direc-
tors, and producers. Visit the SAG's Web site for more information.
Screen Actors Guild (SAG)
5757 Wilshire Boulevard
Los Angeles, CA 90036-3600
Tel: 323-954-1600
http://www.sag.com

For information about opportunities in not-for-profit theaters,
contact:
Theatre Communications Group
520 Eighth Avenue, 24th Floor
New York, NY 10017-4156
Tel: 212-609-5900
Email: tcg@tcg.org
http://www.tcg.org

This site has information for beginners on acting and the acting
business.
Acting Workshop On-Line
http://www.redbirdstudio.com/AWOL/acting2.html

Animators

OVERVIEW

Animators are artists who design the cartoons that appear in movies, television shows, and commercials. Approximately 94,000 animators and multimedia artists are employed in the United States.

HISTORY

Frenchman Emile Reynaud created what is considered the first animated cartoon in 1892. He created the cartoon by drawing and hand-painting images on film paper and using a praxinoscope, an optical instrument he invented to create the illusion of movement, otherwise known as animation. *Fantasmagorie*, considered the first fully animated film, was made by French director Emile Courtet (aka Emile Cohl) in 1908.

As Hollywood grew in the early 1900s, so did companies that created cartoons, although these animated films were silent (just like all movies of the time). Bray Studios in New York City was one of the best-known cartoon studios of the time. It operated from circa 1915 to the late 1920s. Some of its cartoons include *Out of the Inkwell* (1916), *Electric Bell* (1918), and *If You Could Shrink* (1920).

Walt Disney also got his start in the business around this time. In 1923, he sold his first cartoon, *Alice's Wonderland,* to a distributor and soon after founded Disney Brothers Cartoon Studio (later renamed Walt Disney Studio) with his brother, Roy. By the late 1920s, "talkies" had replaced silent films, and Walt Disney had created the cartoon character Mickey Mouse, which entertains young and old to this day.

QUICK FACTS

School Subjects
Art
Computer science

Personal Skills
Artistic
Communication/ideas

Work Environment
Primarily indoors
Primarily one location

Minimum Education Level
High school diploma

Salary Range
$29,610 to $76,690 to $94,080+

Certification or Licensing
None available

Outlook
About as fast as the average

DOT
141

GOE
01.02.03

NOC
5241

O*NET-SOC
27-1014.00

The 1930s and 1940s are considered the golden age of animation. The Walt Disney Studio dominated the industry during these decades. During this time, it created the first animated feature film, *Snow White and the Seven Dwarfs*—which debuted in 1937. The animated film was so groundbreaking that the Academy of Motion Pictures and Sciences gave it a special award in 1938, stating: "to Walt Disney for *Snow White and the Seven Dwarfs,* recognized as a significant screen innovation which has charmed millions and pioneered a great new entertainment field for the motion picture cartoon." Walt Disney Studio went on to create many other animated feature-length classics, including *Pinocchio, Fantasia,* and *Dumbo.*

The popularity of television in the 1950s caused a decline in interest in theatrical cartoons and feature films that lasted into the 1980s. Many consider the release of *Who Framed Roger Rabbit?* by Walt Disney Studio in 1988 as the beginning of a renaissance in animation that continues to this day. Major animation trends over the last two decades include the popularity of adult-oriented animation, such as *The Simpsons* and *South Park*; the emergence of *anime* [Japanese-based (although the phenomena has spread throughout Asia), high-quality animation in a variety of genres geared not just toward children but adults, too]; the creation of cable networks such as Nickelodeon and the Cartoon Network, which offer animation as much or all of their programming; and the rise of computer-generated animation, which allows animators infinite creative options and the ability to complete animated features in far less time than by using traditional methods.

THE JOB

Animators, often called *motion cartoonists,* design the cartoons that appear in films and television shows. They also create the digital effects for many films and commercials. Computer animators created more than 2,000 of the effects in *Star Wars: Episode I—The Phantom Menace.* Making a big-budget animated film such as *A Bug's Life* or *Shrek* requires a team of many creative people. Each animator on the team works on one small part of the film. On a small production, animators may be involved in many different aspects of the project's development.

An animated film begins with a script. *Screenwriters* plan the story line (plot) and write it with dialogue and narration. *Designers* read the script and decide how the film should look—should it be realistic, futuristic, or humorous? They then draw some of the characters and backgrounds. These designs are then passed on to a *storyboard artist* who illustrates the whole film in a series of frames, similar to a very long comic strip. Based on this storyboard, an artist can then create a detailed layout.

The most common form of animation is *cell animation.* Animators examine the script, the storyboard, and the layout and begin to prepare the finished artwork frame by frame, or cell by cell, on a combination of paper and transparent plastic sheets. Some animators create the "key" drawings—the drawings that capture the characters' main expressions and gestures at important parts in the plot. Other animators create the "in between" drawings—the drawings that fill in the spaces between one key drawing and the next. The thousands of final black and white cells are then scanned into a computer. With computer programs, animators add color, special effects, and other details.

In *stop-motion animation,* an object such as a clay creature or doll is photographed, moved slightly, and photographed again. The process is repeated hundreds of thousands of times. Movies such as *Chicken Run* were animated this way. In computer or digital animation, the animator creates all the images directly on the computer screen. Computer programs can create effects such as shadows, reflections, distortions, and dissolves.

Animators are relying increasingly on computers in various areas of production. Computers are used to color animation art, whereas formerly, every frame was painted by hand. Computers also help animators create special effects or even entire films. (One program, Macromedia's Flash, has given rise to an entire Internet cartoon subculture.)

Other people who work in animation are *prop designers*, who create objects used in animated films, and *layout artists*, who visualize and create the world that cartoon characters inhabit.

REQUIREMENTS

High School

If you are interested in becoming an animator, you should, of course, take art as well as computer classes in high school. Math classes such as algebra and geometry will also be helpful. If your school offers graphic design classes, be sure to take those.

Postsecondary Training

You do not need to go to college to become an animator, but there are a number of animation programs offered at universities and art institutes across the country. You may choose to pursue an associate's, bachelor's, master's of fine art, or a Ph.D. in computer animation, digital art, graphic design, or art. Some of today's top computer animators are self-taught or have learned their skills on the job.

Other Requirements

Animators must be creative. In addition to having artistic talent, they must generate ideas, although it is not unusual for animators to collaborate with writers for ideas. They must have a good sense of humor (or a good dramatic sense) and an observant eye to detect people's distinguishing characteristics and society's interesting attributes or incongruities.

Animators need to be flexible. Because their art is commercial, they must be willing to accommodate their employers' desires if they are to build a broad clientele and earn a decent living. They must be able to take suggestions and rejections gracefully.

EXPLORING

Ask your high school art or computer teacher to arrange a presentation by an animator, or if you live near an animation studio, try to arrange a tour of a production facility. Sketch as much as you possibly can. Carry a sketchpad around in order to quickly capture images and gestures that seem interesting to you. There are many computer animation software programs available that teach basic principles and techniques. Experiment with these programs to create basic animation. Some video cameras have stop-motion buttons that allow you to take a series of still shots. You can use this feature to experiment with claymation and other stop-motion techniques.

EMPLOYERS

Approximately 94,000 animators and multimedia artists are employed in the United States. Employers of animators include producers, movie studios, and television networks. In addition, a number of these artists are self-employed, working on a freelance basis. Some do animation on the Web as a part-time business or hobby. Others work for computer game companies.

STARTING OUT

A few employers, such as the Walt Disney Studio, offer apprenticeships. To enter these programs, applicants must have attended an accredited art school for two or three years.

One new way that up-and-coming animators have made themselves known to the animating community is by attracting an audience on the World Wide Web. A portfolio of well-executed Web 'toons can help an animator build his or her reputation and get jobs. Some animators, such as the Brothers Chaps (creators of http://homestarrunner.com), have even been able to turn their creations into a profitable business.

ADVANCEMENT

Animators' success, like that of other artists, depends on how much the public likes their work. Very successful animators work for well-known film companies and other employers at the best wages; some become well known to the public.

EARNINGS

According to the U.S. Department of Labor, multimedia artists and animators employed in the motion picture and video industries earned an annual mean salary of $76,690 in 2004. Salaries for all multimedia artists and animators ranged from less than $29,610 to more than $94,080. Cell painters, as listed in a salary survey conducted by *Animation World,* start at about $750 a week; animation checkers, $930 a week; and story sketchers, $1,500 weekly.

Self-employed artists do not receive fringe benefits such as paid vacations, sick leave, health insurance, or pension benefits. Those who are salaried employees of companies and the like do typically receive these fringe benefits, however.

WORK ENVIRONMENT

Most animators work in big cities where movie and television studios are located. They generally work in comfortable environments with good light. Staff animators work a regular 40-hour workweek but may occasionally be expected to work evenings and weekends to meet deadlines. Freelance animators have erratic schedules, and the number of hours they work may depend on how much money they want to earn or how much work they can find. They often work evenings and weekends but are not required to be at work during regular office hours.

Animators can be frustrated by employers who curtail their creativity, asking them to follow instructions that are contrary to what they would most like to do. Many freelance animators spend a lot of time working alone at home, but animators have more opportunities to interact with other people than do most working artists.

OUTLOOK

Employment for artists and related workers is expected to grow about as fast as the average for all occupations through 2014, according to the U.S. Department of Labor. The growing trend of sophisticated special effects in motion pictures should create opportunities at industry-effects houses such as Sony Pictures Imageworks, Dream-Quest Software, Industrial Light & Magic, and DreamWorks SKG. Furthermore, growing processor and Internet connection speeds are creating a Web-animation renaissance. Because so many creative and talented people are drawn to this field, however, competition for jobs will be strong.

Animated features are not just for children anymore. Much of the animation today is geared toward an adult audience. Interactive computer games, animated films, network and cable television, and the Internet are among the many employment sources for talented animators. More than 60 percent of all visual artists are self-employed, but freelance work can be hard to come by, and many freelancers earn little until they acquire experience and establish a good reputation. Competition for work will be keen; those with an undergraduate or advanced degree in art or film will be in demand. Experience in action drawing and computers is a must.

FOR MORE INFORMATION

For membership and scholarship information, contact
International Animated Film Society
2114 Burbank Boulevard
Burbank, CA 91506-1232
Tel: 818-842-8330
Email: asifaalert-subscribe@yahoogroups.com
http://www.asifa-hollywood.org

For an art school directory, a scholarship guide, and general information, contact
National Art Education Association
1916 Association Drive
Reston, VA 20191-1590
Tel: 703-860-8000

Email: naea@dgs.dgsys.com
http://www.naea-reston.org

For an overview of animation and useful exercises, visit the following Web site:
Animating: Creating Movement Frame by Frame
http://www.oscars.org/teachersguide/animation/download.html

Art Directors

OVERVIEW

In films, videos, and television commercials, *art directors* set the general look of the visual elements and approve the props, costumes, and models. In addition, they are involved in casting, editing, and selecting the music. In film (motion pictures) and video, the art director is usually an experienced animator or computer/graphic arts designer who supervises animators or other artistic staff. They supervise both in-house and off-site staff, handle executive issues, and oversee the entire artistic production process. There are approximately 71,000 art directors working in the United States.

HISTORY

Artists have always been an important part of the creative process throughout history. Medieval monks illuminated their manuscripts, painting with egg-white tempera on vellum. Each copy of each book had to be printed and illustrated individually.

Printed illustrations first appeared in books in 1461. Through the years, prints were made through woodblock, copperplate, lithography, and other means of duplicating images. Although making many copies of the same illustration was now possible, publishers still depended on individual artists to create the original works. Text editors usually decided what was to be illustrated and how, while artists commonly supervised the production of the artwork.

The first art directors were probably staff illustrators for book publishers. As the publishing industry grew more complex and incorporated new technologies such as photography and film, art

QUICK FACTS

School Subjects
Art
Computer science

Personal Skills
Artistic
Communication/ideas

Work Environment
Primarily indoors
Primarily one location

Minimum Education Level
Bachelor's degree

Salary Range
$36,660 to $73,190 to
$122,400+

Certification or Licensing
None available

Outlook
About as fast as the average

DOT
164

GOE
01.02.03

NOC
5131

O*NET-SOC
27-1011.00

direction evolved into a more supervisory position and became a full-time job. Publishers and advertisers began to need specialists who could acquire and use illustrations and photos.

With the creation of animation, art directors became more indispensable than ever. Animated short films, such as the early Mickey Mouse cartoons, were usually supervised by art directors. Walt Disney, himself, was the art director on many of his early pictures. And as full-length films have moved into animation, the sheer number of illustrations requires more than one art director to oversee the project.

Today's art directors supervise almost every type of visual project produced. Through a variety of methods and media, from television and film to magazines, comic books, and the Internet, art directors communicate ideas by selecting and supervising every element that goes into the finished product.

THE JOB

Art directors are responsible for all visual aspects of on-screen or printed projects. The art director oversees the process of developing visual solutions to a variety of communication problems. He or she creates film and video productions, television commercials, and Web sites; helps to establish corporate identities; advertises products and services; and enhances books, magazines, newsletters, and other publications. Some art directors with experience or knowledge in specific fields specialize in such areas as packaging, exhibitions and displays, or the Internet. But all directors, even those with specialized backgrounds, must be skilled in and knowledgeable about design, illustration, photography, computers, research, and writing in order to supervise the work of graphic artists, photographers, copywriters, text editors, and other employees.

In film and video and broadcast advertising, the art director has a wide variety of responsibilities and often interacts with an enormous number of creative professionals. Working with directors, producers, and other professionals, art directors interpret scripts and create or select settings in order to visually convey the story or the message. The art director oversees and channels the talents of set decorators and designers, model makers, location managers, propmasters, construction coordinators, and special effects people. In addition, art directors work with writers, unit production managers, cinematographers, costume designers, and postproduction staff, including editors and employees responsible for scoring and titles. The art director is ultimately responsible for all visual aspects of the finished product.

The process of producing the look of a motion picture or a television show begins in much the same way that a printed advertising piece is created. The art director may start with the director or producer's concept or create one in-house in collaboration with staff members. Once a concept has been created, the art director sketches a rough storyboard based on the director or producer's ideas, and the plan is presented for review to those involved. The next step is to develop a finished storyboard, with larger and more detailed frames (the individual scenes) in color. This storyboard is presented to the client for review and used as a guide for the film director as well.

Technology is playing an increasingly important role in the art director's job. Most art directors, for example, use a variety of computer software programs, including Adobe PageMaker, FrameMaker, Illustrator, and Photoshop; Macromedia Dreamweaver; QuarkX-Press; and CorelDRAW. Many others create and oversee Web sites for clients and work with other interactive media and materials, including CD-ROM, touch-screens, multidimensional visuals, and new animation programs.

Art directors usually work on more than one project at a time and must be able to keep numerous, unrelated details straight. They often work under pressure of a deadline and yet must remain calm and pleasant when dealing with clients and staff. Because they are supervisors, art directors are often called upon to resolve problems, not only with projects but with employees as well.

Art directors are not entry-level workers. They usually have years of experience working at lower-level jobs in the field before gaining the knowledge needed to supervise projects. Depending on whether they work primarily in film, television, or publishing, art directors have to know how film is processed or digitally mastered or how printing presses operate. They should also be familiar with a variety of production techniques in order to understand the wide range of ways that images can be manipulated to meet the needs of a project.

REQUIREMENTS
High School
A college degree is usually a requirement for art directors; however, in some instances, it is not absolutely necessary. A variety of high

school courses will give you both a taste of college-level offerings and an idea of the skills necessary for art directors on the job. These courses include art, drawing, art history, graphic design, illustration, photography, advertising, and desktop publishing.

Other useful courses that you should take in high school include business, computing, drama, English, technical drawing, cultural studies, psychology, and social science.

Postsecondary Training

Courses in photography, filmmaking, set direction, advertising, marketing, layout, desktop publishing, and fashion are also important for those interested in becoming art directors. Specialized courses, sometimes offered only at professional film or art schools, may be particularly helpful for students who want to go into art direction. These include animation, storyboard, typography, Web site design, and portfolio development.

Because of the rapidly increasing use of computers in design work, it is essential to have a thorough understanding of how computer art and layout programs work. In smaller companies, the art director may be responsible for operating this equipment; in larger companies, a staff person, under the direction of the art director, may use these programs. In either case, the director must know what can be done with the available equipment.

In addition to course work at the college level, many universities and professional art schools offer graduates or students in their final year a variety of workshop projects, desktop publishing training opportunities, and internships. These programs provide students with opportunities to develop their personal design styles as well as their portfolios.

Other Requirements

The work of an art director requires creativity, imagination, curiosity, and a sense of adventure. Art directors must be able to work with all sorts of specialized equipment and computer software, such as graphic design programs, as well as make presentations on the ideas behind their work.

The ability to work well with different people and organizations is a must for art directors. They must always be up to date on new techniques, trends, and attitudes. And because deadlines are a constant part of the work, an ability to handle stress and pressure well is key.

Other requirements for art directors include time management skills and an interest in media and people's motivations and lifestyles.

EXPLORING

High school students can get an idea of what an art director does by working on the staff of the school newspaper, magazine, or yearbook, and developing their own Web sites or zines. It may also be possible to secure a part-time job assisting the advertising director of the local newspaper or to work at an advertising agency. Developing your own artistic talent is important, and this can be accomplished through self-training (reading books and practicing); through courses in painting, drawing, or other creative arts; or by working with a group of friends to create a movie. At the very least, you should develop your "creative eye" (that is, your ability to develop ideas visually). One way to do this is by familiarizing yourself with great works, such as paintings or highly creative motion pictures, videos, or commercials.

EMPLOYERS

Approximately 71,000 art directors are employed in the United States. A variety of organizations in virtually all industries employ art directors. Art directors who oversee and produce on-screen products often work for film and television production houses, Web designers, multimedia developers, computer games developers, or television stations.

Others might work at advertising agencies, publishing houses, museums, packaging firms, photography studios, marketing and public relations firms, desktop publishing outfits, digital prepress houses, or printing companies.

STARTING OUT

Since an art director's job requires a great deal of experience, it is usually not considered an entry-level position. Typically, a person on a career track toward art director is hired as an assistant to an established director. Recent graduates wishing to enter the field should have a portfolio containing samples of their work to demonstrate their understanding of both the business and the media in which they want to work.

Serving as an intern is a good way to get experience and develop skills. Graduates should also consider taking an entry-level job at a film or television studio or in a publisher's art department to gain initial experience. Either way, aspiring art directors must be willing to acquire their credentials by working on various projects. This may mean working in a variety of areas, such as advertising, marketing, editing, and design.

ADVANCEMENT

While some may be content upon reaching the position of art director to remain there, many art directors take on even more responsibility within their organizations, become film or television directors, start their own advertising agencies, create their own Web sites, develop original multimedia programs, or launch their own magazines.

Many people who get to the position of art director do not advance beyond the title but move on to work on more prestigious films or at better-known firms. Competition for top positions continues to be keen because of the sheer number of talented people interested. At smaller publications or local companies, the competition may be less intense, since candidates are competing primarily against others in the local market.

EARNINGS

According to the U.S. Department of Labor, a beginning art director or an art director working at a small firm can expect to make $36,660 or less per year in 2004, with experienced art directors working at larger companies earning more than $122,400. Mean annual earnings for art directors employed in the motion picture and video industries were $73,190 in 2004.

Most companies employing art directors offer insurance benefits, a retirement plan, and other incentives and bonuses. Freelance art directors employed in the motion picture and television industries are usually responsible for providing their own health insurance and other benefits.

WORK ENVIRONMENT

Art directors usually work in studios or office buildings. While their work areas are ordinarily comfortable, well lit, and ventilated, they often handle glue, paint, ink, and other materials that pose safety hazards, and they should, therefore, exercise caution.

Art directors at art and design studios and publishing firms usually work a standard 40-hour week. Many, however, work overtime during busy periods in order to meet deadlines. Similarly, directors at film and video operations and at television studios work as many hours as required—usually many more than 40 per week—in order to finish projects according to predetermined schedules.

While art directors work independently while reviewing artwork and reading copy, much of their time is spent collaborating with and supervising a team of employees, often consisting of copywriters, editors, photographers, graphic artists, and account executives.

OUTLOOK

The extent to which art director positions are in demand, like many other positions, depends on the economy in general; when times are tough, people and businesses spend less, and cutbacks are made. When the economy is healthy, employment prospects for art directors will be favorable. The U.S. Department of Labor predicts that employment for art directors will grow about as fast as the average for all other occupations through 2014. Creators of films, television shows, and videos need images in order to produce their programs, and people working with new media are increasingly looking for artists and directors to promote new and existing products and services, enhance their Web sites, develop new multimedia programs, and create multidimensional visuals. People who can quickly and creatively generate new concepts and ideas will be in high demand.

However, it is important to note that the supply of aspiring artists is expected to exceed the number of job openings. As a result, those wishing to enter the field will encounter keen competition for salaried, staff positions as well as for freelance work. And although the Internet is expected to provide many opportunities for artists and art directors, some firms are hiring employees without formal art or design training to operate computer-aided design systems and oversee work.

FOR MORE INFORMATION

For more information on design professionals, contact
American Institute of Graphic Arts
164 Fifth Avenue
New York, NY 10010-5901
Tel: 212-807-1990
http://www.aiga.org

The Art Directors Club is an international, nonprofit organization of directors in advertising, graphic design, interactive media, broadcast design, typography, packaging, environmental design, photography, illustration, and related disciplines. For information, contact

Art Directors Club
106 West 29th Street
New York, NY 10001-5301
Tel: 212-643-1440
Email: info@adcglobal.org
http://www.adcglobal.org

For information on the graphic arts, contact
Graphic Artists Guild
90 John Street, Suite 403
New York, NY 10038-3202
Tel: 212-791-3400
http://www.gag.org

Broadcast Engineers

OVERVIEW

Broadcast engineers, also referred to as *broadcast technicians,* or *broadcast operators,* operate and maintain the electronic equipment used to record and transmit the audio for radio signals and the audio and visual images for television signals to the public. They may work in a broadcasting station or assist in broadcasting directly from an outside site as a *field technician.* Approximately 34,000 broadcast engineers work in the United States.

HISTORY

At the end of the 19th century, Guglielmo Marconi (1874–1937), an Italian engineer, successfully sent radio waves across a room in his home and helped launch the 20th-century age of mass communication. Marconi quickly realized the potential for his experiments with radio waves. By 1901 he had established the Marconi Wireless Company in England and the United States and soon after successfully transmitted radio signals across the Atlantic Ocean for the first time.

At first, radio signals were used to transmit information and for communication between two points, but eventually the idea was developed that radio could be used for entertainment, and in 1919, the Radio Corporation of America, or RCA, was founded. Families everywhere gathered around their radios to listen to music, drama, comedy, and news programs. Radio became a commercial success, and radio technology advanced, creating the need for skilled engineers to operate the complicated electronic equipment.

In 1933, frequency modulation, or FM, was introduced; originally there had been only amplitude modulation, or AM. This vastly improved the quality of radio broadcasting. At the same time, experimentation was occurring with higher frequency radio waves, and in 1939 at the World's Fair in New York City, RCA demonstrated television.

The effect television had on changing mass communication was as dramatic as the advent of the radio. Technology continued to advance with the introduction of color imaging, which became widely available in 1953. The number of VHF and UHF channels continued to increase; in the 1970s cable television and subscription television became available, further increasing the amount and variety of programming. Continuing advances in broadcast technology ensure the need for trained engineers who understand and can maintain the highly technical equipment used in television and radio stations.

One of the recent changes in technology that affects broadcast engineers is the switch from analog to digital signals. These changes provide ongoing challenges for television and radio stations.

THE JOB

Broadcast engineers are responsible for the transmission of radio and television programming, including live and recorded broadcasts. Broadcasts are usually transmitted directly from the station; however, engineers are capable of transmitting signals on location from specially designed, mobile equipment. The specific tasks of the broadcast engineer depend on the size of the television or radio station. In small stations, engineers have a wide variety of responsibilities. Larger stations are able to hire a greater number of engineers and specifically delegate responsibilities to each engineer. In both small and large stations, however, engineers are responsible for the operation, installation, and repair of the equipment.

The *chief engineer* in both radio and television is the head of the entire technical operation and must orchestrate the activities of all the technicians to ensure smooth programming. He or she is also responsible for the budget and must keep abreast of new broadcast communications technology.

Larger stations also have an *assistant chief engineer* who manages the daily activities of the technical crew, controls the maintenance of the electronic equipment, and ensures the performance standards of the station.

Maintenance technicians are directly responsible for the installation, adjustment, and repair of the electronic equipment.

Video technicians usually work in television stations to ensure the quality, brightness, and content of the visual images being recorded

Top Radio Formats

1. News/Talk/Information
2. Adult Contemporary
3. Contemporary Hit Radio
4. Urban
5. Rock
6. Hispanic
7. Country
8. Oldies
9. Alternative
10. New AC/Smooth Jazz
11. Religion
12. Adult Standards
13. Classical

Source: Arbitron Format Trends Report, Fall 2002
(Note: Ages 12 and over)

and broadcast. They are involved in several different aspects of broadcasting and videotaping television programs. Technicians who are mostly involved with broadcasting programs are often called *video-control technicians*. In live broadcasts using more than one camera, they operate electronic equipment that selects which picture goes to the transmitter for broadcast. They also monitor on-air programs to ensure good picture quality. Technicians mainly involved with taping programs are often called *videotape-recording technicians*. They record performances on videotape using video cameras and tape-recording equipment, then splice together separate scenes into a finished program; they can create special effects by manipulating recording and re-recording equipment. The introduction of robotic cameras, six-foot-tall cameras that stand on two legs, created a need for a new kind of technician called a *video-robo technician*. Video-robo technicians operate the cameras from a control room computer, using joysticks and a video panel to tilt and focus each camera. With the help of new technology, one person can now effectively perform the work of two or three camera operators. Engineers may work with producers, directors, and reporters to put together videotaped material from various sources. These include networks, mobile camera units, and studio productions. Depending on their employer, engineers may be involved in any number of activities related to editing videotapes into a complete program.

REQUIREMENTS

High School

Take as many classes as you can in mathematics, science, computers, and shop, especially electronics. Speech classes will help you hone your abilities to effectively communicate ideas to others.

Postsecondary Training

Positions that are more advanced require a bachelor's degree in broadcast communications or a related field. To become a chief engineer, you should aim for a bachelor's degree in electronics or electrical engineering. Because field technicians also act as announcers on occasion, speech courses and experience as an announcer in a school radio station can be helpful. Seeking education beyond a bachelor's degree will further the possibilities for advancement, although it is not required.

Certification or Licensing

The Federal Communications Commission licenses and permits are no longer required of broadcast engineers. However, certification from the Society of Broadcast Engineers (SBE) is desirable, and certified engineers consistently earn higher salaries than uncertified engineers. The SBE offers an education scholarship and accepts student members; members receive a newsletter and have access to their job line.

Other Requirements

Broadcast engineers must have both an aptitude for working with highly technical electronic and computer equipment and minute attention to detail to be successful in the field. You should enjoy both the technical and artistic aspects of working in the radio or television industry. You should also be able to communicate with a wide range of people with various levels of technical expertise.

EXPLORING

Reading association publications is an excellent way to learn more about broadcast engineering. Many of the associations listed at the end of this article offer newsletters and other publications to members—some even post back issues or selected articles on their Web sites. You might also consider reading *Broadcast Engineering* (http://www.broadcastengineering.com), a trade publication for broadcast engineers and technicians.

Experience is necessary to begin a career as a broadcast engineer, and volunteering at a local broadcasting station is an excellent way to gain experience. Many schools have clubs for persons interested in broadcasting. Such clubs sponsor trips to broadcasting facilities, schedule lectures, and provide a place where students can meet others with similar interests. Local television station technicians are usually willing to share their experiences with interested young people. They can be a helpful source of informal career guidance. Visits or tours can be arranged by school officials. Tours will allow you to see engineers involved in their work. Most colleges and universities also have radio and television stations where students can gain experience with broadcasting equipment.

Exposure to broadcasting technology also may be obtained through building and operating an amateur, or ham, radio and experimenting with electronic kits. Dexterity and an understanding of home-operated broadcasting equipment will aid in promoting success in education and work experience within the field of broadcasting.

EMPLOYERS

According to the *CIA World Factbook*, there were 13,750 radio stations and 2,218 television stations in the United States in 2006. These stations might be independently operated or owned and operated by a network. Smaller stations in smaller cities are good starting places, but it is at the larger networks and stations in major cities where the higher salaries are found. Some broadcast engineers work outside of the radio and television industries, producing, for example, corporate employee training and sales programs. Approximately 34,000 broadcast technicians are employed in the United States.

STARTING OUT

In many towns and cities there are public-access cable television stations and public radio stations where high school students interested in broadcasting and broadcast technology can obtain an internship. An entry-level technician should be flexible about job location; most begin their careers at small stations and with experience may advance to larger-market stations.

ADVANCEMENT

Entry-level engineers deal exclusively with the operation and maintenance of their assigned equipment; in contrast, a more advanced broadcast engineer directs the activities of entry-level engineers and makes judgments on the quality, strength, and subject of the material being broadcast.

After several years of experience, a broadcast engineer may advance to *assistant chief engineer.* In this capacity, he or she may direct the daily activities of all of the broadcasting engineers in the station as well as the field engineers broadcasting on location. Advancement to chief engineer usually requires at least a college degree in engineering and many years of experience. A firm grasp of management skills, budget planning, and a thorough knowledge of all aspects of broadcast technology are necessary to become the chief engineer of a radio or television station.

EARNINGS

Larger stations usually pay higher wages than smaller stations, and television stations tend to pay more than radio stations. Also, commercial stations generally pay more than public broadcasting stations. The median annual earnings for broadcast technicians were $29,130 in 2004, according to the U.S. Department of Labor. The department also reported that the lowest paid 10 percent earned less than $15,190 and the highest paid 10 percent earned more than $63,180 during that same period. Technicians employed in radio and television broadcasting had mean annual salaries of $31,890 in 2004. Experience, job location, and educational background are all factors that influence a person's pay.

WORK ENVIRONMENT

Most engineers work in broadcasting stations that are modern and comfortable. The hours can vary; because most broadcasting stations operate 24 hours a day, seven days a week, there are engineers who must work at night, on weekends, and on holidays. Transmitter technicians usually work behind the scenes with little public contact. They work closely with their equipment and as members of a small crew of experts whose closely coordinated efforts produce smooth-running programs. Constant attention to detail and having to make split-second decisions can cause tension. Since broadcasts also occur outside of the broadcasting station on location sites, field technicians may work anywhere and in all kinds of weather.

OUTLOOK

According to the U.S. Department of Labor, the overall employment of broadcast technicians is expected to grow about as fast as the average for all occupations through 2014. There will be strong competition for jobs in metropolitan areas. In addition, the Department of Labor predicts that a slow growth in the number of new radio and television stations may mean few new job opportunities in the field. Technicians trained in the installation of transmitters should have better work prospects as television stations switch from their old analog transmitters to digital transmitters. Job openings will also result from the need to replace existing engineers who often leave the industry for other jobs in electronics.

Some engineers may find work outside of broadcasting. As the new technology becomes more accessible, new industries are discovering the usefulness of visual communications. More and more corporations are creating in-house communications departments to produce their own corporate and industrial videos. Videos effectively explain company policies ranging from public safety (aimed at their customers) to first aid (aimed at their employees). Also, high quality, professional videos can introduce a company to potential clients in the best light.

In addition to industrial work, videographers are in great demand today for the production of commercials, animation, and computer graphics. The field of videography is changing rapidly with the introduction of new and cheaper computer systems and desktop software packages. Maintenance workers will always be in demand, even with the new technology. Someone will always have to be on hand to fix broken equipment and to keep new equipment in good working order.

FOR MORE INFORMATION

Visit the BEA's Web site for useful information about broadcast education and the broadcasting industry.
Broadcast Education Association (BEA)
1771 N Street, NW
Washington, DC 20036-2891
Tel: 888-380-7222
Email: beainfo@beaweb.org
http://www.beaweb.org

For information on union membership, contact
National Association of Broadcast Employees and Technicians
Email: nabet@nabetcwa.org
http://nabetcwa.org

For broadcast education, support, and scholarship information, contact
National Association of Broadcasters
1771 N Street, NW
Washington, DC 20036-2891

Tel: 202-429-5300
Email: nab@nab.org
http://www.nab.org

For information on student membership, scholarships, and farm broadcasting, contact
National Association of Farm Broadcasters
PO Box 500
Platte City, MO 64079-0500
Tel: 816-431-4032
Email: nafboffice@aol.com
http://nafb.com

For information on careers in the cable industry, visit the NCTA's Web site.
National Cable and Telecommunications Association (NCTA)
1724 Massachusetts Avenue, NW
Washington, DC 20036-1903
Tel: 202-775-3550
http://www.ncta.com

For scholarship and internship information, contact
Radio-Television News Directors Association and Foundation
1600 K Street, NW, Suite 700
Washington, DC 20006-2838
Tel: 202-659-6510
Email: rtnda@rtnda.org
http://www.rtnda.org

For information on membership, scholarships, and certification, contact
Society of Broadcast Engineers
9102 North Meridian Street, Suite 150
Indianapolis, IN 46260-1896
Tel: 317-846-9000
Email: mclappe@sbe.org
http://www.sbe.org

Visit the society's Web site for information on scholarships, membership for college students, and links to useful resources.
Society of Motion Picture and Television Engineers
3 Barker Avenue
White Plains, NY 10601-1509
Tel: 914-761-1100
http://www.smpte.org

Camera Operators

OVERVIEW

Camera operators use motion picture cameras and equipment to photograph subjects or material for movies, television programs, or commercials. They usually use 35-millimeter or 16-millimeter cameras or camcorders and a variety of films, lenses, tripods, and filters in their work. Their instructions often come from cinematographers or directors of photography. Approximately 28,000 camera operators work in the United States.

HISTORY

Motion pictures were made as early as 1877, using a series of still photographs to create the illusion of motion. But it was Thomas Edison who, in 1889, produced the first single-unit motion picture camera that set the standard for today.

The motion picture industry blossomed in the United States during the 20th century. With the growth of the television industry and the addition of commercial advertising to television, camera operators became indispensable members of the production crew. Motion picture directors and producers rely on camera operators to create the images on film that the directors and producers envision in their minds. As camera equipment becomes more complex and sophisticated, the camera operator will need to be more proficient at his or her craft.

QUICK FACTS

School Subjects
Art
Mathematics

Personal Skills
Communication/ideas
Mechanical/manipulative

Work Environment
Indoors and outdoors
Primarily multiple locations

Minimum Education Level
High school diploma

Salary Range
$16,600 to $38,900 to $75,120+

Certification or Licensing
None available

Outlook
About as fast as the average

DOT
143

GOE
01.02.03

NOC
5222

O*NET-SOC
27-4031.00

THE JOB

Motion picture camera operators may work on feature films in Hollywood or on location elsewhere. Many work on educational films, documentaries, or television programs. The nature of the camera operator's work depends largely on the size of the production crew. If the film is a documentary or short news segment, the camera operator may be responsible for setting up the camera and lighting equipment as well as for supervising the actors during filming. Equipment that camera operators typically use includes cranes, dollies, mounting heads, and different types of lenses and accessories. Often, the camera operator is also responsible for maintenance and repair of all of this equipment.

With a larger crew, the camera operator is responsible only for the actual filming. The camera operator may even have a support team of assistants. The *first assistant camera operator* will typically focus on the cameras, making sure cameras are loaded and operating correctly and conferring with lighting specialists. In larger productions, there are also backup cameras and accessories for use if one should malfunction during filming. *Second assistant camera operators* help the first assistant set up scenes to be filmed and assist in the maintenance of the equipment.

Sometimes camera operators must use shoulder-held cameras. This often occurs during the filming of action scenes for television or motion pictures. *Special effects camera operators* photograph the optical effects segments for motion pictures and television. They create visual illusions that can add mood and tone to the motion picture. They usually add fades, dissolves, superimpositions, and other effects to their films at the request of the *director of photography*, also known as the *director of cinematography* or the *cinematographer*.

Brian Fass is a cinematographer/camera assistant in New York City. On a project, he works closely with the other professionals to help establish a visual style for the film. "During the project," he says, "I work on setting up the camera in various positions for coverage of scenes and then lighting each chosen angle." Fass has worked as a camera assistant for the Woody Allen films *Everyone Says I Love You* and *Deconstructing Harry,* as well as the Sidney Lumet film *Gloria.*

REQUIREMENTS

High School

Take classes that will prepare you for the technical aspect of the work—courses in photography, journalism, and media arts should give you some hands-on experience with a camera. Mathematics and science can help you understand cameras and filters. You should also take art and art history classes and other courses that will help you develop appreciation of visual styles.

Postsecondary Training

A college degree is not necessary to get a position as a camera operator, but a film school can help you expand your network of connections. A bachelor's degree in liberal arts or film studies provides a good background for work in the film industry, but practical experience and industry connections will provide the best opportunities for work. Upon completing an undergraduate program, you may wish to enroll in a master's program at a film school. Schools offering well-established programs include the School of Visual Arts in New York, New York University, and the University of Southern California. These schools have film professionals on their faculties and provide a very visible stage for student talent, being located in the two film business hot spots-New York and California. Film school offers overall formal training, providing an education in fundamental skills by working with student productions. Such education is rigorous, but in addition to teaching skills it provides you with peer groups and a network of contacts with students, faculty, and guest speakers that can be of help after graduation.

Other Requirements

You must be able to work closely with other members of a film crew and to carefully follow the instructions of the cinematographer and other camera operators. Since lighting is an integral part of filmmaking, you should have a thorough understanding of lighting equipment in order to work quickly and efficiently. In addition to the technical aspects of filmmaking, you should also understand the artistic nature of setting up shots. "I'm dyslexic and have always gravitated toward the visual mediums," Brian Fass says. "I feel that this impairment, along with my love of movies, made me turn toward cinematography."

EXPLORING

You should join a photography or camera club, or become involved with the media department of your school. You may have the opportunity then to videotape sports events, concerts, and school plays. You can also learn about photography by working in a camera shop. A part-time job in a camera shop will give you a basic understanding of photographic equipment. Some school districts have television stations where students can learn the basics of camera operation. This kind of hands-on experience is invaluable when it comes time to find work in the field. You can also learn about the film industry by reading such publications as *American Cinematographer* (http://www. theasc.com/magazine) and *Cinefex* (http://www.cinefex.com).

Top Cable Networks, 2006

Rank	Network	Subscribers
1	Discovery	92,300,000
2	ESPN	92,200,000
3	CNN (Cable News Network)	92,000,000
3	USA Network	92,000,000
5	TNT (Turner Network Television)	91,900,000
6	Lifetime Television (LIFE)	91,800,000
7	Weather Channel	91,700,000
7	ESPN2	91,700,000
7	Nickelodeon	91,700,000
10	Spike TV	91,600,000
10	A&E Networks	91,600,000
12	TBS	91,500,000
13	The Learning Channel (TLC)	91,400,000
14	CNN Headline News	91,200,000
15	MTV	91,100,000
16	Home and Garden Television (HGTV)	91,000,000
16	C-SPAN (Cable Satellite Public Access Network)	91,000,000
16	ABC Family Channel	91,000,000
19	History Channel	90,900,000
19	Cartoon Network	90,900,000

Source: Kagan Research, LLC

EMPLOYERS

There are approximately 28,000 television, video, and movie camera operators working in the United States. About one in five of these operators is self-employed. The majority of camera operators who are salaried employees work for the film and television industry at TV stations or film studios. Most jobs are found in large, urban areas.

STARTING OUT

Most entry-level jobs require little formal preparation in photography or camera operation. A college degree is not required by most film or television studios, but you may have to belong to the International Alliance of Theatrical Stage Employees (IATSE) Local 600, the national union for camera operators. An entry-level job as a camera assistant usually begins with assignments such as setting up or loading film into cameras and adjusting or checking lighting. With experience, the assistant may participate in decisions about what to photograph or how to film a particular scene.

Before you receive any paying jobs, you may have to work awhile as a volunteer or intern on a film project. You can surf the Internet for postings of openings on film productions, or contact your state's film commission.

ADVANCEMENT

It usually takes two to four years for a motion picture camera operator to learn the techniques necessary for the job. Those who become proficient in their field, after several years of training, may be able to work on film projects as a cinematographer or director of photography (DP). The DP supervises other camera operators and works more closely with the directors, producers, and actors in the creation of the film. Some camera operators study cinematography part-time while keeping their jobs as camera operators. They may later move to larger studios or command higher salaries. Camera operators who are employed in the television industry might advance by working on more prestigious projects, working for larger stations, or by managing the work of other camera operators.

"I work as an assistant for the money," Brian Fass says, "but hope to jump into work as a DP full time if the jobs come along. I also own my own Aaton XTR camera package, which makes me more marketable for DP jobs."

EARNINGS

Self-employed camera operators typically work on a project-by-project basis and may have periods of unemployment between jobs. Those working on movies may be paid per-day, and their role in the creation of the movie may last anywhere from several weeks to several months. Camera operators who are salaried employees of a television network, for example, have steady, year-round employment. Because of these factors and others, such as area of the country in which the operator works and the size of the employer, salaries vary widely for these professionals. The U.S. Department of Labor reports the median annual earnings of all television, video, and motion picture camera operators as $38,900 in 2004. The department also reports that the lowest paid 10 percent of operators earned less than $16,600 per year, but at the top

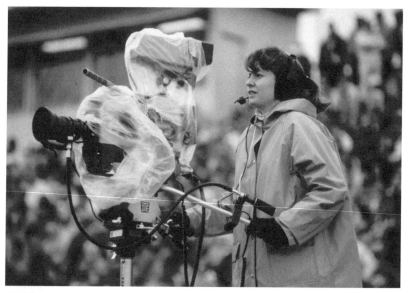

Camera operators sometimes work outdoors in inclement weather.
(Jim Whitmer Photography)

end of the pay scale, the highest earning 10 percent made more than $75,120 annually.

Salaried employees usually receive benefits such as health insurance, retirement plans, and vacation days. Those who are self-employed must pay for such extras themselves.

WORK ENVIRONMENT

Camera operators work indoors and outdoors. Most work for motion picture studios or in television broadcasting. During filming, a camera operator may spend several weeks or months on location in another city or country. Most often, the camera operator lives and works in his or her home city and works during regular business hours. Hours can be erratic, however, if the film includes scenes that must be shot at night, or if a deadline must be met by after-hours filming.

Much of the work of a camera operator becomes routine after a few years of experience. Camera operators get used to loading and unloading film, carrying cameras and equipment from trucks or workshops into studios or sets, and filming segments over and over again. The glamour of working on motion pictures or television programs may be diminished by the physically demanding work.

Also, the actors, directors, and producers are the individuals in the limelight. They often receive credit for the work the camera operators have done.

Many camera operators must be available to work on short notice. Since motion picture camera operators are generally hired to work on one film at a time, there may be long periods during which a camera operator is not working. Few can make a living as self-employed camera operators.

Camera operators working on documentary or news productions may work in dangerous places. Sometimes they must work in uncomfortable positions or make adjustments for imperfect lighting conditions. They usually operate their cameras while standing hours at a time. Deadline pressure is also a constant in the camera operator's work. Working for directors or producers who are on tight budgets or strict schedules may be very stressful.

OUTLOOK

Employment for camera operators is expected to increase about as fast as the average for all occupations through 2014, according to the U.S. Department of Labor. The use of visual images continues to grow in areas such as communication, education, entertainment, marketing, and research and development. More businesses will make use of video training films and public relations projects that use film. Camera operators will also be needed to help create made-for-the-Internet broadcasts. The entertainment industries are also expanding. However, competition for positions is very fierce. Employment will not be as strong in television broadcasting as automation reduces the number of camera operators needed to create television shows, newscasts, and other productions. Camera operators work in a desirable and exciting field, and they must work hard and be aggressive to get good jobs, especially in Los Angeles and New York.

FOR MORE INFORMATION

For lists of tricks of the trade and favorite films of famous cinematographers, visit the ASC' s Web site.

American Society of Cinematographers (ASC)
PO Box 2230
Hollywood, CA 90078-2230
Tel: 800-448-0145
Email: info@theasc.com
http://www.theasc.com

For information on membership benefits, contact this branch of the International Alliance of Theatrical Stage Employees (IATSE):
International Cinematographers Guild (IATSE Local 600)
National Office/Western Region
7755 Sunset Boulevard
Hollywood, CA 90046-3911
Tel: 323-876-0160
http://www.cameraguild.com

For information on union membership, contact
National Association of Broadcast Employees and Technicians
Email: nabet@nabetcwa.org
http://nabetcwa.org

Visit the society's Web site for information on scholarships, membership for college students, and links to useful resources.
Society of Motion Picture and Television Engineers
3 Barker Avenue
White Plains, NY 10601-1509
Tel: 914-761-1100
http://www.smpte.org

Visit this Web site organized by the ASC for a list of film schools and to learn about the career of cinematographer—the next step on the career ladder for camera operators.
Cinematographer.com
http://www.cinematographer.com

Disc Jockeys

OVERVIEW

Disc jockeys (DJs) play recorded music for radio stations or for parties, dances, and special events. On the radio, they intersperse the music with a variety of advertising material and informal commentary. They may also perform such public services as announcing the time, the weather forecast, travel times, or important news. Interviewing guests and making public service announcements may also be part of the DJ's work.

HISTORY

Guglielmo Marconi, a young Italian engineer, first transmitted a radio signal in his home in 1895. Radio developed rapidly as people began to comprehend its tremendous possibilities. The stations KDKA in Pittsburgh and WWWJ in Detroit began broadcasting in 1920. Within 10 years, there were radio stations in all the major cities in the United States and broadcasting had become big business. The National Broadcasting Company became the first network in 1926 when it linked together 25 stations across the country. The Columbia Broadcasting System was organized the following year. In 1934, the Mutual Broadcasting Company was founded. The years between 1930 and 1950 may be considered the zenith of the radio industry. With the coming of television, radio broadcasting took second place in importance as entertainment for the home, but radio's commercial and communications value should not be underestimated.

The first major contemporary disc jockey in the United States was Alan Freed, who worked in the 1950s on WINS radio in New York. In 1957, his rock and roll stage shows at the Paramount Theater made front-page news in *The New York Times* because of the huge crowds they attracted. The title "disc jockey" arose when most music was recorded on conventional flat records or discs.

Today, much of the recorded music used in commercial radio stations is on magnetic tape, compact disc, or digital files. The disc jockey personalities are still very much a part of the radio station's image, with major players commanding top salaries.

THE JOB

Disc jockeys serve as a bridge between the music itself and the listener. They also perform such public services as announcing the time, the weather forecast, or important news. Working at a radio station can be a lonely job, since often the DJ is the only person in the studio. But because their job is to maintain the good spirits of their audience and attract new listeners, disc jockeys must possess the ability to sound relaxed and cheerful.

Dave Wineland is a disc jockey at WRZQ 107.3 in Columbus, Indiana. He once worked the popular 5:30 A.M. to 10:00 A.M. shift that many commuters listen to on their way to work but now works the afternoon shift. Like many DJs, his duties extend beyond on-the-air announcements. He also works as production director at the station and writes and produces many of the commercials and promotion announcements. "I spend a lot of time in the production room," says Wineland, who also delegates some of the production duties to other DJs on the staff.

Unlike the more conventional radio or television announcer, the disc jockey is not bound by a written script. Except for the commercial announcements, which must be read as written, the DJ's statements are usually spontaneous. They are not usually required to play a musical selection to the end; they may fade out a record when it interferes with a predetermined schedule for commercials, news, time checks, or weather reports. DJs are not always free to play what they want; at some radio stations, especially the larger ones, the program director or the music director makes the decisions about the music that will be played. And while some stations may encourage their disc jockeys to talk, others emphasize music over commentary and restrict the amount of ad-libbing by DJs.

Many DJs have become well-known public personalities in broadcasting; they may participate in community activities and public events.

Disc jockeys who work at parties and other special events usually work on a part-time basis. They are often called *party DJs*. A DJ

A disc jockey listens to an audio cut during a commercial break. (*Jim Whitmer Photography*)

who works for a supplying company receives training, equipment, music, and job assignments from the company. Self-employed DJs must provide everything they need themselves. Party DJs have more contact with people than do radio DJs, so they must be personable with clients.

REQUIREMENTS

High School

In high school, you can start to prepare for a career as a disc jockey. A good knowledge of the English language, correct pronunciation, and diction are important. High school English classes as well as speech classes are helpful in getting a good familiarity with the language. Extracurricular activities such as debating and theater will also help with learning good pronunciation and projection. Music classes will introduce you to musical styles, techniques, and artists.

Some high schools have radio stations on site where students can work as DJs, production managers, or technicians. This experience can be a good starting point to learn more about the field. Dave Wineland's first radio job was at the radio station at Carmel High School in Indianapolis.

Postsecondary Training

Although there are no formal educational requirements for becoming a disc jockey, many large stations prefer applicants with a college education. Some students choose to attend a school specifically for broadcasting, taking courses specific to becoming an announcer. However, students should research the school's reputation by getting references from the school or the local Better Business Bureau. Many other hopeful DJs obtain a more general degree in communications. Like many disc jockeys today, Wineland has a college degree. He earned a degree in telecommunications from Ball State University.

Although there may not be any specific training program required by prospective employers, station officials pay particular attention to taped auditions of the applicant. Companies that hire DJs for parties will often train them; experience is not always necessary if the applicant has a suitable personality.

Other Requirements

Disc jockeys should be levelheaded and able to react calmly even in the face of a crisis. Many unexpected circumstances can arise that demand the skill of quick thinking. For example, if guests who are to appear on a program either do not arrive or become too nervous to go on the air, the DJ must fill the airtime. He or she must also smooth over a breakdown in equipment or some other technical difficulty.

Union membership may be required for employment with large stations in major cities. The largest talent union is the American Federation of Television and Radio Artists. Many small stations, however, hire nonunion workers.

EXPLORING

Reading publications will help you learn more about the radio industry. *Radio & Records* (in print and online at http://www.radioandrecords.com) is one of the most popular publications for those involved in the radio business. It contains news on radio happenings, formats, a directory of organizations and services related to the field, and job listings.

If a career as a DJ sounds interesting, you might try to get a summer job at a radio station. Although you may not get a chance to work on air, working behind the scenes will allow you to gauge whether or not such work appeals to you.

Take advantage of any opportunity you get to speak or perform before an audience. Appearing as a speaker or a performer can help you decide whether or not you have the necessary stage presence for a career on the air.

Many colleges and universities have their own radio stations and offer courses in radio. Students can gain valuable experience working at college-owned stations. Some radio stations offer students financial assistance and on-the-job training in the form of internships and co-op work programs, as well as scholarships and fellowships.

EMPLOYERS

There has been a steady growth in the number of radio stations in the United States. According to the *CIA World Factbook*, there were 13,750 radio stations in the United States in 2006.

Radio is a 24-hour-a-day, seven-day-a-week medium, so there are many slots to fill. Most of these stations are small, so disc jockeys are required to perform many other duties for a lower salary than at larger stations in bigger metropolitan areas.

As a result of the Telecommunications Act of 1996, companies can own an unlimited number of radio stations nationwide with an eight-station limit within one market area, depending on the size of the market. When this legislation took effect, mergers and acquisitions changed the face of the radio industry. So, while the pool of employers is smaller, the number of stations continues to rise.

STARTING OUT

One way to enter this field is to apply for an entry-level job rather than a job as a disc jockey. It is also advisable to start at a small local station. As opportunities arise, DJs commonly move from one station to another.

While still a high school student, Dave Wineland applied for a position at his local radio station in Monticello, Indiana. "I was willing to work long hours for low pay," he says, acknowledging that starting out in radio can require some sacrifices. However, on-air experience is a must.

An announcer is employed only after an audition. Audition material should be selected carefully to show the prospective employer the range of the applicant's abilities. A prospective DJ should practice talking aloud, alone, and then make a tape of him- or herself with five to seven minutes of material to send to radio stations. The tape should include a news story, two 60-second commercials, and a sample of the applicant introducing and coming out of a record. (Tapes should not include the whole song, just the first and final few seconds, with the aspiring DJ introducing and finishing the music; this is called "telescoping.") In addition to presenting prepared materials, applicants may also be asked to read material that they have not seen previously. This may be a commercial, news release, dramatic selection, or poem.

ADVANCEMENT

Most successful disc jockeys advance from small stations to large ones. The typical experienced DJ will have held several jobs at different types of stations.

Some careers lead from being a DJ to doing other types of radio or television work. More people are employed in sales, promotion, and planning than in performing, and they are often paid more than DJs.

EARNINGS

The salary range for disc jockeys is extremely broad, with the lowest 10 percent of DJs earning less than $6.22 an hour, or $12,940 a year in 2004, according to the U.S. Department of Labor, and a high of more than $1,000,000 for popular broadcast personalities such as Howard Stern. The average salary in 2004 was $22,820, according to the U.S. Department of Labor.

Top Radio Markets, 2006

1. New York, N.Y.	6. Houston-Galveston, Tex.
2. Los Angeles, Calif.	7. Philadelphia, Pa.
3. Chicago, Ill.	8. Washington, D.C.
4. San Francisco, Calif.	9. Atlanta, Ga.
5. Dallas-Ft. Worth, Tex.	10. Detroit, Mich.

Source: Arbitron

Smaller market areas and smaller stations fall closer to the bottom of the range, while the top markets and top-rated stations offer DJs higher salaries.

Benefits vary according to the size of the market and station. However, vacation and sick time is somewhat limited because the medium requires that radio personalities be on the air nearly every day.

WORK ENVIRONMENT

Work in radio stations is usually very pleasant. Almost all stations are housed in modern facilities. Temperature and dust control are important factors in the proper maintenance of technical electronic equipment, and people who work around such machinery benefit from the precautions taken to preserve it.

The work can be demanding. It requires that every activity or comment on the air begin and end exactly on time. This can be difficult, especially when the disc jockey has to handle news, commercials, music, weather, and guests within a certain time frame. It takes a lot of skill to work the controls, watch the clock, select music, talk with a caller or guest, read reports, and entertain the audience; often, several of these tasks must be performed simultaneously. A DJ must be able to plan ahead and stay alert so that when one song ends, he or she is ready with the next song or with a scheduled commercial.

Because radio audiences listen to DJs who play the music they like and talk about the things that interest them, DJs must always be aware of what pleases their audience. If listeners begin switching stations, ratings go down and disc jockeys can lose their jobs.

Disc jockeys do not always have job security; if the owner or manager of a radio station changes, the DJ may lose his or her job. The consolidation of radio stations to form larger, cost-efficient stations has caused some employees to lose their jobs.

DJs may work irregular hours. They may have to report for work at very early hours in the morning. Sometimes they will be free during the daytime hours but will have to work late into the night. Many radio stations operate on a 24-hour basis. All-night announcers may be alone in the station during their working hours.

The disc jockey who stays with a station for a period of time becomes a well-known personality in the community. Such celebrities are sought after as participants in community activities and may be recognized on the street.

DJs who work at parties and other events work in a variety of settings. They generally have more freedom to choose music selections but little opportunity to ad-lib. Their work is primarily on evenings and weekends.

OUTLOOK

According to the National Association of Broadcasters, radio reaches 78 percent of all consumers every day. Despite radio's popularity, the *Occupational Outlook Handbook* projects that employment of announcers will decline slightly through 2014. As a result of this decline, competition for jobs will be great in an already competitive field.

While small stations will still hire beginners, on-air experience will be increasingly important. Another area where job seekers can push ahead of the competition is in specialization. Knowledge of specific areas such as business, consumer, and health news may be advantageous.

While on-air radio personalities are not necessarily affected by economic downturns, mergers and changes in the industry can affect employment. If a radio station has to make cuts due to a weak economy, it will most likely do so in a behind-the-scenes area, which means that the disc jockeys who remain may face a further diversity in their duties. On the other hand, the growth of satellite radio has created additional opportunities for disc jockeys.

Fewer positions may also be available to disc jockeys in the future due to voice-tracking, which is the prerecording of a radio show by a DJ for one or more shifts in one or more cities. Voice-tracking saves radio companies money by allowing the work of one DJ to be used in a variety of settings and time slots. Of course, voice-tracking cannot be used for talk shows, remote broadcasts, or live concerts. The industry is divided on how this new trend will affect the radio industry on the whole. However, the consolidation of radio stations and use of voice-tracking is likely to cause the number of DJ jobs to decline.

FOR MORE INFORMATION

Visit the BEA's Web site for useful information about broadcast education and the broadcasting industry.
Broadcast Education Association
1771 N Street, NW
Washington, DC 20036-2891
Tel: 888-380-7222
Email: beainfo@beaweb.org
http://www.beaweb.org

For broadcast education, support, and scholarship information, contact
National Association of Broadcasters
1771 N Street, NW
Washington, DC 20036-2891
Tel: 202-429-5300
Email: nab@nab.org
http://www.nab.org

For scholarship and internship information, contact
Radio-Television News Directors Association and Foundation
1600 K Street, NW, Suite 700
Washington, DC 20006-2838
Tel: 202-659-6510
Email: rtnda@rtnda.org
http://www.rtnda.org

For career information and an overview of the industry, visit
About.com: Radio
http://radio.about.com

Lighting Technicians

OVERVIEW

Lighting technicians set up and control lighting equipment for television broadcasts, taped television shows, motion pictures, and video productions. They begin by consulting with the production director and technical director to determine the types of lighting and special effects that are needed. Working with spot and flood lights, mercury-vapor lamps, white and colored lights, reflectors (mainly employed out of doors), and a large array of dimming, masking, and switching controls, they light scenes to be broadcast or recorded.

HISTORY

For centuries before the arrival of electric lights, theaters used candles and oil lamps to make the action on an indoor stage visible. The effects produced were necessarily limited by the lack of technology. In 1879, Thomas A. Edison developed a practical electric light bulb by removing most of the oxygen from a glass bulb and then sending current through a carbon filament inside—producing a light that would not burn out. With the arrival of electric lights, it was only a short time before theater lighting became more sophisticated; spotlights and various lighting filters were put to use, and specialists in lighting emerged.

The manipulation of light and shadow is one of the basic principles of filmmaking. This was particularly the case during the era of the silent film; without sound, filmmakers relied upon images to tell their stories. Lighting professionals learned how to make the illusion complete; through expert lighting, cardboard backdrops could substitute for the outdoors, actors could change appearance, and cheaply constructed costumes could look extravagant. Lighting technicians were the first visual-effects masters, using tricks with light to achieve realism. As film techniques and equipment evolved, lighting technicians worked with cinematographers and directors to create the dark recesses and gritty streets of the film noir, the lavish spectacle of the movie musical, and the sweeping plains of the American western, often within the confines of a studio. In the 1960s and 1970s, however, a new movie realism called for lighting technicians to expose, with uneven lighting and weak light sources, all the imperfections they'd been covering up before. Today, in the era of the special effects blockbuster, lighting technicians have gone back to their roots, using light and advanced equipment to make model cities, planets, and monsters look real.

THE JOB

Whenever a movie or television show is filmed, the location must be well lit, whether indoors in a studio or outdoors on location. Without proper lighting, the cameras would not be able to film properly, and the show would be difficult to watch. Lighting technicians set up and control the lighting equipment for movie and television productions. These technicians are sometimes known as *assistant chief set electricians* or *lights operators*.

When beginning a project, lighting technicians consult with the director to determine the lighting effects needed; then they arrange the lighting equipment and plan the light-switching sequence that will achieve the desired effects. For example, if the script calls for sunshine to be streaming in through a window, they will set up lights to produce this effect. Other effects they may be asked to produce include lightning, the flash from an explosion, or the soft glow of a candle-lit room.

For a television series, which uses a similar format for each broadcast, the lights often remain in one fixed position for every show. For a one-time production, such as a scene in a movie, the lights have to be physically set up according to the particular scene.

During filming, lighting technicians follow a script that they have marked or follow instructions from the technical director. The script tells them which lighting effects are needed at every point in the filming. In a television studio, lighting technicians watch a monitor screen to check the lighting effects. If necessary they may alter the lighting as the scene progresses by adjusting controls in the control room.

Broadcasts from indoor settings require carrying and setting up portable lights. In small television stations, this work may be done by the camera operator or an assistant. In a large station, or in any big movie or television production, a lighting technician may supervise several assistants as they set up the lights.

Even outdoor scenes require lighting, especially to remove shadows from people's faces. For outdoor scenes in bad weather or on rough terrain, it may be a difficult task to secure the lighting apparatus firmly so that it is out of the way, stable, and protected. During a scene, whether broadcast live or recorded on film, lighting technicians must be able to concentrate on the lighting of the scene and must be able to make quick, sure decisions about lighting changes.

There are different positions within this field, depending on experience. A lighting technician can move up into the position of *best boy* (the term applies to both genders). This person assists the *chief lighting technician,* or *gaffer.* The gaffer is the head of the lighting department and hires the lighting crew. Gaffers must be sure the filmed scene looks the way the director and the director of photography want it to look. They must diagram each scene to be filmed and determine where to position each light and decide what kinds of lights will work best for each particular scene. Gaffers must be observant, noticing dark and bright spots and correcting their light levels before filming takes place.

REQUIREMENTS

High School

You should learn as much as possible about electronics in high school. Physics, mathematics, and any shop courses that introduce electronics equipment provide a good background. You should also take courses that will help you develop computer skills needed for operating lighting and sound equipment. Composition or technical writing courses can give you the writing skills you'll need to communicate ideas to other technicians.

Postsecondary Training

There is strong competition for broadcast and motion picture technician positions, and, in general, only well-prepared technicians get good jobs. You should attend a two-year postsecondary training program in electronics and broadcast technology, especially if you hope to advance to a supervisory position. Film schools also offer useful degrees in production, as do theater degrees. For a position as a chief engineer, a bachelor's degree is usually required.

Other Requirements

Setting up lights can be heavy work, especially when lighting a large movie set. You should be able to handle heavy lights on stands and work with suspended lights while on a ladder. Repairs such as changing light bulbs or replacing worn wires are sometimes necessary. You should be able to work with electricians' hand tools (screwdrivers, pliers, and so forth) and be comfortable working with electricity. You should also be dependable and capable of working as part of a team. Communications skills, both listening and speaking, are necessary when working with a director and with assistant light technicians.

EXPLORING

Valuable learning experiences for prospective lighting technicians include working on the lighting for a school stage production, building a radio from a kit, or attaining summer job in an appliance or TV or computer repair shop. High school shop or vocational teachers may be able to arrange a presentation by a qualified lighting technician.

You can also learn a lot about the technical side of production by operating a camera for your school's journalism or media department. Videotaping a play, concert, or sporting event will give you additional insight into production work. You may also have the opportunity to intern or volunteer with a local technical crew for a film or TV production. Check the Internet for production schedules, or volunteer to work for your state's film commission where you'll hear about area projects.

EMPLOYERS

Many lighting technicians work on a freelance basis, taking on film, TV, and commercial projects as they come along. Technicians can find full-time work with large theater companies and television broadcast stations, or any organization, such as a museum or sports arena, that requires special lighting. Lighting technicians also work for video production companies.

STARTING OUT

The best way to get experience is to find a position as an intern. Offering to work for a production for course credit or experience instead of pay will enable you to learn about the job and to establish valuable connections. Most people interested in film and television enter the industry as production assistants. These positions are often unpaid and require a great deal of time and work with little reward. However, production assistants have the opportunity to network with people in the industry. They get to speak to lighting technicians and to see them at work. Once they've worked on a few productions, and have learned many of the basics of lighting, they can negotiate for paid positions on future projects.

ADVANCEMENT

An experienced lighting technician will be able to move up into the position of best boy. With a few more years' experience working under different gaffers on diverse projects, the technician may move into the position of gaffer or chief lighting technician. Gaffers command greater salaries as they gain experience working with many different cinematographers. Many experienced technicians join the International Alliance of Theatrical Stage Employees, Moving Picture Technicians, Artists and Allied Crafts (IATSE) as lighting technicians or studio mechanics; union membership is required for work on major productions. Some lighting technicians go on to work as cinematographers or to make their own films or television movies.

EARNINGS

Salaries for lighting technicians vary according to the technician's experience. Annual income is also determined by the number of projects a technician is hired for; the most experienced technicians can work year-round on a variety of projects, while those starting out may go weeks without work. According to IATSE, the minimum hourly pay for unionized gaffers was $22.50 in 2000. Unionized best boys and other lighting technicians earned at least $16.50 to $20.50 an hour. Experienced technicians can negotiate for much higher wages. Union members are also entitled to certain health and retirement benefits.

WORK ENVIRONMENT

Lighting technicians employed in television normally work a 40-hour week and change jobs only as their experience makes advancement possible. Technicians employed in the motion picture industry are often employed for one production at a time and thus may work less regularly and under a more challenging variety of conditions than light technicians in television studio work.

Technicians often work long days, especially when a film is on a tight schedule or when news teams are covering a late-breaking story. Technicians may travel a good deal to be on location for filming. They work both indoors in studios and outdoors on location, under a variety of weather conditions.

OUTLOOK

As long as the movie and television industries continue to grow, opportunities will remain available for people who wish to become lighting technicians. With the expansion of the cable market, lighting technicians may find work in more than one area. However, persistence and hard work are required in order to secure a good job in film or television.

The increasing use of visual effects and computer generated imagery (CGI) will likely have an impact on the work of lighting technicians. Through computer programs, filmmakers and editors can adjust lighting themselves; however, live-action shots are still integral to the filmmaking process and will remain so for some time. To get the initial shots of a film will require sophisticated lighting equipment and trained technicians. Lighting technicians often have to know about the assembly and operation of more pieces of equipment than anyone else working on a production. Equipment will become more compact and mobile, making the technician's job easier.

FOR MORE INFORMATION

For information about colleges with film and television programs of study, and to read interviews with filmmakers, visit the AFI's Web site.

American Film Institute (AFI)
2021 North Western Avenue
Los Angeles, CA 90027-1657
Tel: 323-856-7600
http://www.afi.com

Visit the ASC's Web site for a great deal of valuable insight into the industry, including interviews with award-winning cinematographers, a "tricks of the trade" page, information about film schools, multimedia presentations, and the American Cinematographer *online magazine.*

American Society of Cinematographers (ASC)
PO Box 2230

Hollywood, CA 90078-2230
Tel: 800-448-0145
Email: info@theasc.com
http://www.theasc.com

For education and training information, check out the following Web site:
  International Alliance of Theatrical Stage Employees, Moving
    Picture Technicians, Artists and Allied Crafts
  1430 Broadway, 20th Floor
  New York, NY 10018-3348
  Tel: 212-730-1770
  http://www.iatse-intl.org

Media Planners and Buyers

OVERVIEW

Media specialists are responsible for placing advertisements that will reach targeted customers and get the best response from the market for the least amount of money. Within the media department, *media planners* gather information about the sizes and types of audiences that can be reached through each of the various media and about the cost of advertising in each medium. *Media buyers*, sometimes called *advertising sales agents*, purchase space in printed publications, as well as time on radio or television stations. Advertising media workers are supervised by a *media director,* who is accountable for the overall media plan. In addition to advertising agencies, media planners and buyers work for large companies that purchase space or broadcast time. There are approximately 154,000 advertising sales agents employed in the United States.

HISTORY

The first formal media that allowed advertisers to deliver messages about their products or services to the public were newspapers and magazines, which began selling space to advertisers in the late 19th century. This system of placing ads gave rise to the first media planners and buyers, who were in charge of deciding what kind of advertising to put in which publications and then actually purchasing the space.

In the broadcast realm, radio stations started offering program time to advertisers in the early 1900s. And, while television advertising began just before the end of World War II, producers were quick to realize that they could reach huge audiences by placing ads on TV. Television advertising proved to be beneficial to the TV stations as well, since they relied on sponsors for financial assistance in order to bring programs into people's homes. In the past, programs were sometimes named not for the host or star of the program but for the sponsoring company that was paying for the broadcast of that particular show.

During the early years of radio and television, it was often possible for one sponsor to pay for an entire 30-minute program. The cost of producing shows on radio and television, however, increased dramatically, requiring many sponsors to support a single radio or television program. Media planners and buyers learned to get more for their money by buying smaller amounts of time—60-, 30-, and even 10-second spots—on a greater number of programs.

Today's media planners and buyers have a wide array of media from which to choose. The newest of these, the World Wide Web, allows advertisers not only to precisely target customers but to interact with them as well. In addition to Web banner ads, producers can also advertise via sponsorships, their own Web sites, CD catalogs, voice-mail telephone shopping, and more. With so many choices, media planners and buyers must carefully determine target markets and select the ideal media mix in order to reach these markets at the least cost.

THE JOB

While many employees may work in the media department, the primary specialists are the media planner and the media buyer. They work with professionals from a wide range of media—from billboards, direct mail, and magazines to television, radio, and the Internet. Both types of media specialists must be familiar with the markets that each medium reaches, as well as the advantages and disadvantages of advertising in each.

Media planners determine target markets based on their clients' advertising approaches. Considering their clients' products and services, budget, and image, media planners gather information about the public's viewing, reading, and buying habits by administering questionnaires and conducting other forms of market research. Through this research, planners are able to identify target markets by sorting data according to people's ages, incomes, marital status, interests, and leisure activities.

By knowing which groups of people watch certain shows, listen to specific radio stations, or read particular magazines or newspapers, media planners can help clients select air time or print space to reach the consumers most likely to buy their products. For example, Saturday morning television shows attract children, while late-night programs often draw young singles. For shows broadcast at these times, media planners will recommend air time to their clients who are interested in advertising a certain type of movie to these viewers, such as an animated film or an R-rated comedy, respectively.

Media planners who work directly for companies selling air time or print space must be sensitive to their clients' budgets and resources. When tailoring their sales pitch to a particular client's needs, planners often go to great lengths to persuade the client to buy air time or advertising space. They produce brochures and reports that detail the characteristics of their viewing or reading market, including the average income of those individuals, the number of people who see the ads, and any other information that may be likely to encourage potential advertisers to promote their products.

Media planners try to land contracts by inviting clients to meetings and presentations and educating them about various marketing strategies. They must not only pursue new clients but also attend to current ones, making sure that they are happy with their existing advertising packages. For both new and existing clients, the media planner's main objective is to sell as much air time or ad space as possible.

Media buyers do the actual purchasing of the time on radio or television or the space in a newspaper or magazine in which an advertisement will run. In addition to tracking the time and space available for purchase, media buyers ensure that ads appear when and where they should, negotiate costs for ad placement, and calculate rates, usage, and budgets. They are also responsible for maintaining contact with clients, keeping them informed of all advertising-related developments, and resolving any conflicts that arise. Large companies that generate a lot of advertising or those that place only print ads or only broadcast ads sometimes differentiate between the two main media groups by employing *space buyers* and/or *time buyers*.

Workers who actually sell the print space or air time to advertisers are called *print sales workers* or *broadcast time salespeople*. Like media planners, these professionals are well versed about the target markets served by their organizations and can often provide useful information about editorial content or broadcast programs.

In contrast to print and broadcast planners and buyers, *interactive media specialists* are responsible for managing all critical aspects of their clients' online advertising campaigns. While interactive media planners may have responsibilities similar to those of print or broadcast planners, they also act as new technology specialists, placing and tracking all online ads and maintaining relationships with clients and Webmasters alike.

The typical online media planning process begins with an agency spreadsheet that details the criteria about the media buy. These criteria often include target demographics, start and end dates for the ad campaign, and online objectives. After sending all relevant information to a variety of Web sites, the media specialist receives cost, market, and other data from the sites. Finally, the media specialist places the order and sends all creative information needed to the selected Web sites. Once the order has been placed, the media specialist receives tracking and performance data and then compiles and analyzes the information in preparation for future ad campaigns.

Media planners and buyers may have a wide variety of clients. Film studios, television networks, restaurants, hotel chains, beverage companies, food product manufacturers, and automobile dealers all need to advertise to attract potential customers. While huge companies such as motion picture studios, soft drink manufacturers, major airlines, and vacation resorts pay a lot of money to have their products or services advertised nationally, many smaller firms need to advertise only in their immediate area. Local advertising may come from a health club that wants to announce a special membership rate or from a retail store promoting a sale. Media planners and buyers must be aware of their various clients' advertising needs and create campaigns that will accomplish their promotional objectives.

REQUIREMENTS

High School

Although most media positions, including those at the entry level, require a bachelor's degree, you can prepare for a job as media planner and/or buyer by taking specific courses offered at the high school level. These include business, marketing, advertising, cinematography, radio and television, and film and video. General liberal arts classes, such as economics, English, communications, and journalism, are also important, since media planners and buyers must be able to communicate clearly with both clients and coworkers. In addition, mathematics classes will give you the skills to work accurately with budget figures and placement costs.

Postsecondary Training

Increasingly, media planners and buyers have college degrees, often with majors in marketing or advertising. Even if you have prior work experience or training in media, you should select college classes that provide a good balance of business course work, broadcast and print experience, and liberal arts studies.

Business classes may include economics, marketing, sales, and advertising. In addition, courses that focus on specific media, such as cinematography, film and video, radio and television, and new technologies (like the Internet), are important. Additional classes in journalism, English, and speech will prove helpful as well. Media directors often need to have a master's degree, as well as extensive experience working with the various media.

Other Requirements

Media planners and buyers in broadcasting should have a keen understanding of programming and consumer buying trends, as well as knowledge of each potential client's business. Print media specialists must be familiar with the process involved in creating print ads and the markets reached by various publications. In addition, all media workers need to be capable of maintaining good relationships with current clients, as well as pursuing new clients on a continual basis.

Communication and problem solving skills are important, as are creativity, common sense, patience, and persistence. Media planners and buyers must also have excellent oral, written, and analytical skills, knowledge of interactive media planning trends and tools, and the ability to handle multiple assignments in a fast-paced work environment. Strategic thinking skills, industry interest, and computer experience with both database and word processing programs are also vital.

Top U.S. Advertisers, 2006*

Network TV	Cable TV
1. Procter & Gamble Co.	1. Procter & Gamble Co.
2. General Motors Corp.	2. General Motors Corp.
3. Johnson & Johnson	3. Time Warner
4. Ford Motor Co.	4. GlaxoSmithKline

*by advertising expenditures
Source: *Advertising Age*

EXPLORING

Many high schools and two-year colleges and most four-year colleges have media departments that may include radio stations and public access or cable television channels. In order to gain worthwhile experience in media, you can work for these departments as aides, production assistants, programmers, or writers. In addition, high school and college newspapers and yearbooks often need students to sell advertising to local merchants. Theater departments also frequently look for people to sell ads for performance programs.

In the local community, newspapers and other publications often hire high school students to work part time and/or in the summer in sales and clerical positions for the classified advertising department. Some towns have cable television stations that regularly look for volunteers to operate cameras, sell advertising, and coordinate various programs. In addition, a variety of religious-sponsored activities such as craft fairs, holiday boutiques, and rummage sales can provide you with opportunities to create and place ads and work with the local media in order to get exposure for the events.

EMPLOYERS

Media planners and buyers often work for advertising agencies in large cities, such as Chicago, New York, and Los Angeles. These agencies represent various clients who are trying to sell everything from financial services to dishwasher soap to the latest comedy featuring the hot star of the moment. Other media specialists work directly for radio and television networks, newspapers, magazines, and Web sites selling air time and print space. While many of these media organizations are located in large urban areas, particularly radio and television stations, most small towns put out newspapers and therefore need specialists to sell ad space and coordinate accounts. Approximately 154,000 advertising sales agents work in the United States. Twenty percent of agents work in radio and television broadcasting.

STARTING OUT

More than half of the jobs in print and broadcast media do not remain open long enough for companies to advertise available positions in the classified sections of newspapers. As a result, many media organizations, such as radio and television stations, do not usually advertise job openings in the want ads. Media planners and buyers often hear about available positions through friends, acquaintances, or family members and frequently enter the field as entry-level broadcasting or sales associates. Both broadcasting and sales can provide employees just starting out with experience in approaching and working for clients, as well as knowledge about the specifics of programming and its relation to selling air time.

Advertising agencies sometimes do advertise job openings, both in local and national papers and on the Web. Competition is quite fierce for entry-level jobs, however, particularly at large agencies in big cities.

Print media employees often start working on smaller publications as in-house sales staff members, answering telephones and taking orders from customers. Other duties may include handling classified ads or coordinating the production and placement of small print ads created by in-house artists. While publications often advertise for entry-level positions, the best way to find work in advertising is to send resumes to as many agencies, publications, and broadcasting offices as possible. With any luck, your resume will arrive just as an opening is becoming available.

While you are enrolled in a college program, you should investigate opportunities for internships or on-campus employment in related areas. Your school's career planning center or placement office should have information on such positions. Experience often provides a competitive edge for all job seekers, but it is crucial to aspiring media planners and buyers.

ADVANCEMENT

Large agencies and networks often hire only experienced people, so it is common for media planners and buyers to learn the business at smaller companies. These opportunities allow media specialists to gain the experience and confidence they need to move up to more advanced positions. Jobs at smaller agencies and television and radio stations also provide possibilities for more rapid promotion than those at larger organizations.

Media planners and buyers climbing the company ladder can advance to the position of media director or may earn promotions to executive-level positions. For those already at the management level, advancement can come in the form of larger clients and more responsibility. In addition, many media planners and buyers who have experience with traditional media are investigating the opportunities and challenges that come with the job of interactive media planner/buyer or Web media specialist.

EARNINGS

Because media planners and buyers work for a variety of organizations all across the country and abroad, earnings can vary greatly. Media directors can earn between $46,000 and $118,400, depending on the type of employer and the director's experience level. For example, directors at small agencies make an average of $42,100, while those at large agencies can earn more than $120,000, according to a 2002 *Advertising Age* salary survey.

Media planners and buyers in television typically earn higher salaries than those in radio. In general, however, beginning broadcasting salespeople usually earn between $18,000 and $35,000 per year and can advance to as much as $46,000 after a few years of experience.

According to the U.S. Department of Labor, advertising sales agents had salaries that ranged from less than $20,640 to more than $89,290 in 2004. Advertising sales agents employed in radio and television broadcasting had mean annual earnings of $49,580 in 2004; those employed in the motion picture and video industries earned $55,780.

Most employers of media planners and buyers offer a variety of benefits, including health and life insurance, a retirement plan, and paid vacation and sick days.

WORK ENVIRONMENT

Although media planners and buyers often work a 40-hour week, their hours are not strictly nine to five. Service calls, presentations, and meetings with ad space reps and clients are important parts of the job that usually have a profound effect on work schedules. In addition, media planners and buyers must invest considerable time investigating and reading about trends in programming, buying, and advertising.

The variety of opportunities for media planners and buyers results in a wide diversity of working conditions. Larger advertising agencies, publications, and networks may have modern and comfortable working facilities. Smaller markets may have more modest working environments.

Whatever the size of the organization, many planners seldom go into the office and must call in to keep in touch with the home organization. Travel is a big part of media planners' responsibilities to their clients, and they may have clients in many different types of businesses and services, as well as in different areas of the country.

While much of the media planner and buyer's job requires interaction with a variety of people, including coworkers, sales reps, supervisors, and clients, most media specialists also perform many tasks that require independent work, such as researching and writing reports. In any case, the media planner and buyer must be able to handle many tasks at the same time in a fast-paced, continually changing environment.

OUTLOOK

The employment outlook for media planners and buyers, like the outlook for the advertising industry itself, depends on the general health of the economy. When the economy thrives, companies produce an increasing number of goods and seek to promote them via television, radio, the Internet, newspapers, magazines, and various other media. The U.S. Department of Labor anticipates that employment in the advertising industry is projected to grow 22 percent over the 2004-2014 period, faster than the average for all industries.

More and more people are relying on radio and television for their entertainment and information. With cable and local television channels offering a wide variety of programs, advertisers are increasingly turning to TV in order to get exposure for their products and services. Although newspaper sales are in decline, there is growth in special interest periodicals and other print publications. Interactive media such as the Internet, CD catalogs, and voice-mail shopping are providing a flurry of advertising activity all around the world. All of this activity will increase market opportunities for media planners and buyers.

Employment possibilities for media specialists are far greater in large cities, such as New York, Los Angeles, and Chicago, where most magazines and many broadcast networks have their headquarters. However, smaller publications are often located in outlying areas, and large national organizations usually have sales offices in several cities across the country.

Competition for all advertising positions, including entry-level jobs, is expected to be intense. Media planners and buyers who have considerable experience will have the best chances of finding employment.

FOR MORE INFORMATION

For information on college chapters, internship opportunities, and financial aid opportunities, contact
American Advertising Federation
1101 Vermont Avenue, NW, Suite 500
Washington, DC 20005-6306
Tel: 202-898-0089

Email: aaf@aaf.org
http://www.aaf.org

For information on advertising agencies, contact
American Association of Advertising Agencies
405 Lexington Avenue, 18th Floor
New York, NY 10174-1801
Tel: 212-682-2500
http://www.aaaa.org

For career resources and job listings, contact
American Marketing Association
311 South Wacker Drive, Suite 5800
Chicago, IL 60606-6629
Tel: 800-262-1150
Email: info@ama.org
http://www.marketingpower.com

For information on education and training, contact
Marketing Research Association
110 National Drive, 2nd Floor
Glastonbury, CT 06033-1212
Tel: 860- 682-1000
Email: email@mra-net.org
http://www.mra-net.org

Production Assistants

OVERVIEW

Production assistants perform a variety of tasks for television, film, and video producers and other staff members. They must be prepared to help out everywhere, ensuring that daily operations run as smoothly as possible. Some production assistants may perform substantive jobs such as reviewing scripts, but others may primarily run errands. They must be willing to work hard and keep long hours at times, since tight production schedules require full days. An agreeable temperament and willingness to follow instructions and perform simple tasks are very important skills for work in this field.

HISTORY

In the early 20th century, as motion pictures were first developing, the roles of director and producer were combined in one person. European filmmakers such as Georges Melies and Leon Gaumont and New Yorker Edwin S. Porter directed, filmed, and produced very short movies. The first woman to become a director and producer was Alice Guy, who started the Solax Company in New York in 1910. The film industry settled in Hollywood and began to consolidate in the first two decades of this century, as jobs were differentiated. Major studios assembled large staffs, so all stages of production from conception to financing and directing could be performed within a single studio. Twentieth Century Fox, for example, had producers, writers, directors, and actors on staff to choose from for each film. Small producers were forced out of business as major studios grew to have a monopoly on the industry.

In the 1950s, the dominance of major studios in film production was curbed by an antitrust court decision, and more independent producers were able to find projects. Changes in the United States tax code made independent producing more profitable. At the same time, the growth of television provided new opportunities for producers, not only for television films but also for news programs, weekly entertainment programs, sports broadcasts, talk shows, and documentaries. More recently, the video industry, particularly in the areas of music and education, has opened up even more production jobs.

The industry is becoming increasingly international; many foreign-made films and videos are now financed by Americans, and a number of American motion picture companies are under foreign ownership. Currently, many producers work on a project-by-project basis. Independent producers must be good salespersons to market a project to a television or movie studio and to other financial backers. They will try to involve popular actors and media personalities with the project from its inception in order to attract a studio's interest. Studios hire production assistants to facilitate the work of the producer and other staff members.

THE JOB

The work of a production assistant is not glamorous, but production is the best place to learn about the television and film industries. All hiring, casting, and decision making is done by members of production; they are involved with a project from the very beginning through its final stages. The *producer* is in charge—he or she is responsible for coordinating the activities of all employees involved in a production. Producers oversee the budget, and they have the final word on most decisions made for a film or television show.

The responsibilities of production assistants (PAs) range from making sure the star has coffee in the morning to stopping street traffic so a director can film a scene. They photocopy the script for actors, assist in setting up equipment, and perform other menial tasks. The best PAs know where to be at the right time to make themselves useful. Production can be stressful; time is money and mistakes can be very costly. Assistants must be prepared to handle unforeseen problems, smooth out difficulties, and help out as quickly as possible.

Duties may include keeping production files in order. These files will include contracts, budgets, page changes (old pages from a script that has been revised), and other records. The documents must be kept organized and accessible for whenever the producer may need them.

Production assistants may also have to keep the producer's production folder in order and up to date. The production folder contains everything the producer needs to know about the production at a glance. It is particularly useful for times when a producer is on location away from the studio and cannot access the office files. PAs make sure that the folder includes the shooting schedule, the most recent version of the budget, cast and crew lists with phone numbers, a phone sheet detailing all production-related phone calls the producer needs to make, and an up-to-date shooting script. As new versions of these forms are created, PAs update the producer's folder and file the older versions for reference.

PAs may also be in charge of making sure that the producer gets the dailies, the film shot each day. They schedule an hour or so in a producer's schedule to watch the dailies and to make related calls to discuss them with other staff members.

PAs perform a number of other administrative and organizational tasks. They make travel reservations, arrange hotel accommodation, and arrange for rehearsal space. They run errands and communicate messages for producers, directors, actors, musicians, and other members of the technical crew.

PAs who work in television studios for live shows, such as news programs and talk shows, record news feeds, answer phones, operate teleprompters, coordinate tapes, and assist editors. They assist with booking guests and arranging interviews.

Production assistant is the lowest position on the television or film crew. It is an entry-level job that gives someone interested in film and broadcast media the experience and contacts to move into other areas of the industry. PAs often get stuck with undesirable tasks like sweeping floors, guarding sets, or finding a particular brand of green tea for a demanding diva. However, a television, film, or video production would not happen without production assistants on the set or in the studio.

REQUIREMENTS
High School
To work in the television or film industry, you should have an understanding of the artistic and technical aspects of production, as well as a broad knowledge of the industry itself. Take courses in photography, broadcast journalism, and media to learn about cameras and sound equipment. Take courses in art and art history to learn about visual composition, and English to develop communication skills. Business and accounting courses can help you prepare for the bookkeeping requirements of office work.

Postsecondary Training

There are no formal education requirements for production assistants. Most people in the industry consider the position a stepping stone into other careers in the industry. You'll learn much of what you'll need to know on the set of a television production or film, following the instructions of crew members and other assistants. Though a film-school education can't guarantee entry into the business, it can give you an understanding of the industry and help you make some connections. Many film students work part time or on a contract basis as production assistants to gain experience while they are still in school. There are more than 500 film-studies programs offered by schools of higher education throughout the United States. According to the American Film Institute, the most reputable are: Columbia University in New York City, New York University, the University of California at Los Angeles, and the University of Southern California. You may choose to major in English or theater as an undergraduate, then apply to graduate film schools. There are many good undergraduate programs in film and video with concentrations in such areas as directing, acting, editing, producing, screenwriting, cinematography, broadcast engineering, and television. Some people break into the business without formal training by volunteering on as many television or film productions as they can, getting to know professionals in the business, and making valuable connections in the industry. Your chances of moving up, however, are better if you have a college degree.

Other Requirements

Production assistants need agreeable personalities and a willingness to follow instructions and perform simple tasks. You need to catch on quickly to the things you're taught. Organizational skills will help you keep track of the many different aspects of a production. Great ambition and dedication are very important, as getting paying jobs on a production will require persistence. Also, you won't get a great deal of recognition for your hours of work, so you need a sense of purpose and an understanding that you are "paying your dues." A love of television, video, and movies and a fascination with the industry, particularly an interest in the technical aspects of film-making, will help you keep focused. Though you need an outgoing personality for making connections on a production, you should be capable of sitting quietly on the sidelines when not needed.

EXPLORING

There are many ways to gain experience with filmmaking. Some high schools have film clubs and classes in film or video. Experience in theater can also be useful. To learn more, you can work as a volunteer for a local theater or a low-budget film project; these positions are often advertised in local trade publications. You may also be able to volunteer with your state's film commission, helping to solicit production companies to do their filming in the state.

Students interested in production work should read as much as possible about the film and television industry, starting at a school or public library. Trade journals can be very helpful as well; the two most prominent ones are *Daily Variety* (http://www.variety.com) and *Hollywood Reporter* (http://www.hollywoodreporter.com). These resources will have information about production studios that will prove very useful for prospective PAs. *The Rundown* (http://www.tvrundown.com) has information on the television news industry as well as career guidance information. If you are interested in video production, read *Studio/monthly* (http://www.studiodaily.com/studiomonthly).

EMPLOYERS

Production assistants are hired by film and video production companies for individual projects. Some assistants are employed full time in the main offices of a production company or as personal assistants to producers or executives. Production assistants can also find full-time employment at television studios.

STARTING OUT

Look for internships, which may offer course credit if they are unpaid, by reading trade journals and contacting television and film studios. You can also find production opportunities listed on the Internet or through your state's film commission. To gain experience, you may have to work for free on some of your first productions to make contacts within the industry. Since this is an entry-level position, opportunities will open as other assistants advance.

ADVANCEMENT

Production assistant positions are usually temporary. After one or two years, production assistants have enough experience to move into other jobs, and there are numerous choices, depending on their interests. They may wish to go into editing, camera operation, lighting, sound, writing, directing, producing, or performing. All of these areas have a hierarchy of positions that allow a production assistant to work his or her way up to the top jobs. A production assistant can, for example, become a *line producer,* who works closely with the producer, signing checks, advising on union rules, and negotiating deals with studio personnel. An associate producer performs similar work. Becoming a producer or director requires years of experience and hard work.

EARNINGS

Because working as a production assistant is the starting point for most professionals and artists in the television and film industries, many people volunteer their time until they make connections and move into paid positions. Those assistants who can negotiate payment may make between $200 and $400 a week, but they may only have the opportunity to work on a few projects a year. Production assistants working full time in an office may start at around $20,000 a year but with experience can make around $65,000. Full-time production assistants may belong to the Office and Professional Employees International Union, which negotiates salaries. Experienced script supervisors, production office coordinators, and continuity coordinators have the opportunity to join Local #161 of the International Alliance of Theatrical Stage Employees, Moving Picture Technicians, Artists and Allied Crafts of the United States, Its Territories, and Canada. Its members may earn more than $180 a day when working for a production company.

According to Salary.com, production assistants earned a median annual salary of $25,392 in 2006. Salaries ranged from less than $20,307 to $31,802 or more annually.

Those working on a project-to-project basis won't receive any fringe benefits, but those employed full time with a production company can expect health coverage and retirement benefits.

WORK ENVIRONMENT

A television or film set is an exciting environment, but the production assistant may be treated poorly there. With a positive attitude, energy, and a desire to be useful, PAs will earn respect from the production department.

There are unwritten rules that should be followed. A production assistant who works for the producer or for the studio can be seen as an outsider in the eyes of the director and the creative team, so PAs should be respectful and well behaved. This means that production assistants should be quiet, stay out of the way, and avoid touching sets and equipment. If a production assistant behaves as a guest but remains helpful when needed, he or she will earn a good reputation that will be valuable for his or her career advancement.

The work environment will vary; PAs may be required on location or may work mainly in the studio. Production assistants must be willing to work long, demanding hours. Film productions are typically off schedule and over budget, requiring dedication from all those involved. Production assistants and other crew members often go days without seeing family members.

OUTLOOK

There will always be a need for assistants in television and film production. However, since it is such a good entry-level position for someone who wants to make connections and learn about the industry, competition for jobs can be tough. Fortunately, production assistants usually do not stay in their jobs more than one or two years, so turnover is fairly frequent. PAs will find employment anywhere a television show, motion picture, or video is being filmed, but significant opportunities exist in Los Angeles and New York City—the production hubs of the industry. There may be opportunities at local television stations or smaller production companies that produce educational and corporate videos.

FOR MORE INFORMATION

For information about colleges with film and television programs of study and to read interviews with filmmakers, visit the AFI's Web site.

American Film Institute (AFI)
2021 North Western Avenue
Los Angeles, CA 90027-1657
Tel: 323-856-7600
http://www.afi.com

Visit the ASC's Web site for a great deal of valuable insight into the industry, including interviews with award-winning cinematographers, information about film schools, multimedia presentations, and the American Cinematographer *online magazine.*

American Society of Cinematographers (ASC)
PO Box 2230
Hollywood, CA 90078-2230
Tel: 800-448-0145

Email: info@theasc.com
http://theasc.com

For information about career publications, job listings, and industry statistics, contact
National Association of Broadcasters
1771 N Street, NW
Washington, DC 20036-2891
Tel: 202-429-5300
Email: nab@nab.org
http://www.nab.org

For information about careers in cable TV, contact
National Cable and Telecommunications Association
25 Massachusetts Avenue, NW
Washington, DC 20001-1430
Tel: 202-222-2300
http://www.ncta.com

For information on careers, contact
Producers Guild of America
8530 Wilshire Boulevard, Suite 450
Beverly Hills, CA 90211-3115
Tel: 310-358-9020
Email: info@producersguild.org
http://www.producersguild.org

Radio and Television Announcers

OVERVIEW

Radio and television announcers present news and commercial messages from a script. They identify the station, announce station breaks, and introduce and close shows. Interviewing guests, making public service announcements, and conducting panel discussions may also be part of the announcer's work. In small stations, the local announcer may keep the program log, run the transmitter, and cue the changeover to network broadcasting as well as write scripts or rewrite news releases. Approximately 69,000 people are employed as announcers in the United States.

HISTORY

Guglielmo Marconi, a young Italian engineer, first transmitted a radio signal in his home in 1895. Radio developed rapidly as people began to comprehend the tremendous possibilities. The stations KDKA in Pittsburgh and WWWJ in Detroit began broadcasting in 1920. Within 10 years, there were radio stations in all the major cities in the United States, and broadcasting had become big business. The National Broadcasting Company became the first network in 1926 when it linked together 25 stations across the country. The Columbia Broadcasting System was organized in the following year. In 1934, the Mutual Broadcasting Company was founded. The years between 1930 and 1950 may be considered the zenith years of the radio industry. With the advent of television, radio broadcasting took second place in importance as entertainment for the home—but radio's commercial and communications value should not be underestimated.

Discoveries that led to the development of television can be traced as far back as 1878, when William Crookes invented a tube that produced the cathode ray. Other inventors who contributed to the development of television were Vladimir Zworykin, a Russian-born scientist who came to this country at the age of 20 and is credited with inventing the iconoscope before he was 30; Charles Jenkins, who invented a scanning disk, using certain vacuum tubes and photoelectric cells; and Philo Farnsworth, who invented an image dissector. WNBT and WCBW, the first commercially licensed television stations, went on the air in 1941 in New York. Both suspended operations during World War II but resumed them in 1946 when television sets began to be manufactured on a commercial scale.

As radio broadcasting was growing across the country in its early days, the need for announcers grew. They identified the station and brought continuity to broadcast time by linking one program with the next as well as participating in many programs. In the early days (and even today in smaller stations), announcers performed a variety of jobs around the station. When television began, many radio announcers and newscasters started to work in the new medium. The need for men and women in radio and television broadcasting has continued to grow. Television news broadcasting requires specialized on-camera personnel—anchors, television news reporters, broadcast news analysts, consumer reporters, and sports reporters (sportscasters).

THE JOB

Some announcers merely announce; others do a multitude of other jobs, depending on the size of the station. But the nature of their announcing work remains the same.

An announcer is engaged in an exacting career. The necessity for finishing a sentence or a program at a precisely planned moment makes this a demanding and often tense career. It is absolutely essential that announcers project a sense of calm to their audiences, regardless of the activity and tension behind the scenes.

The announcer who plays recorded music interspersed with a variety of advertising material and informal commentary is called a *disc jockey*. This title arose when most music was recorded on conventional flat records or discs. Today much of the recorded music used in commercial radio stations is on magnetic tape or compact discs and other digital media. Disc jockeys serve as a bridge between the music itself and the listener. They may perform such public services as announcing the time, the weather forecast, or important news. It can be a lonely job, since many disc jockeys are the only person in the studio. But because their job is to maintain the good spirits of their audience and to attract new listeners, disc jockeys must possess the ability to be relaxed and cheerful. (For more information on this career, see the article **Disc Jockeys.**)

Unlike the more conventional radio or television announcer, the disc jockey is not bound by a written script. Except for the commercial announcements, which must be read as written, the disc jockey's statements are usually spontaneous. Disc jockeys usually are not required to play a musical selection to the end; they may fade out a record when it interferes with a predetermined schedule for commercials, news, time checks, or weather reports.

Announcers who cover sports events for the benefit of the listening or viewing audience are known as *sportscasters*. This is a highly specialized form of announcing, as sportscasters must have extensive knowledge of the sports that they are covering, plus the ability to describe events quickly and accurately. (For more information on this career, see the article **Sports Broadcasters and Announcers.**)

Often the sportscaster will spend several days with team members, observing practice sessions, interviewing people, and researching the history of an event or of the teams to be covered. The more information that a sportscaster can acquire about individual team members, company they represent, tradition of the contest, ratings of the team, and community in which the event takes place, the more interesting the coverage is to the audience.

The announcer who specializes in reporting the news to the listening or viewing public is called a *newscaster*. This job may require simply reporting facts, or it may include editorial commentary. Newscasters may be given the authority by their employers to express their opinions on news items or the philosophies of others. They must make judgments about which news is important and which is not. In some instances, they write their own scripts based on facts furnished by international news bureaus. In other instances, they read text exactly as it comes in over a teletype machine or teleprompter. They may make as few as one or two reports each day if they work on a major news program, or they may broadcast news for five minutes every hour or half-hour. Their delivery is usually dignified, measured, and impersonal.

The *anchor* generally summarizes and comments on one aspect of the news at the end of the scheduled broadcast. This kind of announcing differs noticeably from that practiced by the sportscaster, whose manner may be breezy and interspersed with slang, or from the disc jockey, who may project a humorous, casual, or intimate image.

The newscaster may specialize in certain aspects of the news, such as economics, politics, or military activity. Newscasters also introduce films and interviews prepared by *news reporters* that provide in-depth coverage and information on the event being reported. *News analysts* are often called *commentators,* and they interpret specific events and discuss how these may affect individuals or the nation. They may have a specified daily slot for which material must be written, recorded, or presented live. They gather information that is analyzed and interpreted through research and interviews and cover public functions such as political conventions, press conferences, and social events.

Smaller television stations may have an announcer who performs all the functions of reporting, presenting, and commenting on the news as well as introducing network and news service reports.

Many television and radio announcers have become well-known public personalities in broadcasting. They may serve as masters of ceremonies at banquets and other public events.

REQUIREMENTS

High School

Although there are no formal educational requirements for entering the field of radio and television announcing, most large stations prefer college-educated applicants. The general reason for this preference is that announcers with broad educational and cultural backgrounds are better prepared to successfully meet a variety of unexpected or emergency situations. The greater his or her knowledge of geography, history, literature, the arts, political science, music, science, and the sound and structure of the English language, the greater the announcer's value.

In high school, therefore, you should focus on a college preparatory curriculum, according to Steve Bell, a professor of telecommunications at Ball State University. A former network anchor who now teaches broadcast journalism, Bell says, "One trend that concerns me is that some high schools are developing elaborate radio and television journalism programs that take up large chunks of academic time, and I think that is getting the cart before the horse. There's nothing wrong with one broadcast journalism course or extracurricular activities, but not at the expense of academic hours."

In that college preparatory curriculum, you should learn how to write and use the English language in literature and communication classes, including speech. Subjects such as history, government, economics, and foreign languages are also important.

Postsecondary Training
When it comes to college, having your focus in the right place is essential, according to Professor Bell. "You want to be sure you're going to a college or university that has a strong program in broadcast journalism, where they also put a strong emphasis on the liberal arts core."

Some advocate a more vocational type of training in preparation for broadcast journalism, but Bell cautions against strictly vocational training. "The ultimate purpose of college is to have more of an education than you have from a trade school. It is important to obtain a broad-based understanding of the world we live in, especially if your career goal is to become an anchor."

A strong liberal arts background with emphasis in journalism, English, political science, or economics is advised, as well as a telecommunications or communications major.

Certification or Licensing
A Federal Communications Commission license or permit is no longer required for broadcasting positions. Union membership may be required for employment with large stations in major cities and is a necessity with the networks. The largest talent union is the American Federation of Television and Radio Artists. Most small stations, however, are nonunion.

Other Requirements
You must have a pleasing voice and personality in order to find success as an announcer. You must be levelheaded and able to react calmly in the face of a major crisis. People's lives may depend on an announcer's ability to remain calm during a disaster. There are also many unexpected circumstances that demand the skill of quick thinking. For example, if guests who are to appear on a program do not arrive or become too nervous to go on the air, you must compensate immediately and fill the airtime. You must smooth over an awkward phrase, breakdown in equipment, or other technical difficulty.

Good diction and English usage, thorough knowledge of correct pronunciation, and freedom from regional dialects are very important. A factual error, grammatical error, or mispronounced word can bring letters of criticism to station managers.

Top Television Markets, 2006

1. New York, N.Y.
2. Los Angeles, Calif.
3. Chicago, Ill.
4. Philadelphia, Pa.
5. Boston, Mass.

6. San Francisco-Oakland-San Jose, Calif.
7. Dallas-Ft. Worth, Tex.
8. Washington, D.C.
9. Atlanta, Ga.
10. Houston-Galveston, Tex.

Source: Nielsen

If you aspire to a career as a television announcer, you must present a good appearance and have no nervous mannerisms. Neatness, cleanliness, and careful attention to the details of proper dress are important. The successful television announcer must have the combination of sincerity and showmanship that attracts and captures an audience.

Broadcast announcing is a highly competitive field. Station officials will pay particular attention to taped auditions of your delivery or, in the case of television, to videotaped demos of sample presentations.

EXPLORING

If you are interested in a career as an announcer, try to get a summer job at a radio or television station. Although you will probably not have the opportunity to broadcast, you may be able to judge whether or not the type of work appeals to you as a career.

Any chance to speak or perform before an audience should be welcomed. Join the speech or debate team to build strong speaking skills. Appearing as a speaker or performer can show whether or not you have the stage presence necessary for a career in front of a microphone or camera.

Many colleges and universities have their own radio and television stations and offer courses in radio and television. You can gain valuable experience working at college-owned stations. Some radio stations, cable systems, and TV stations offer financial assistance, internships, and co-op work programs, as well as scholarships and fellowships.

EMPLOYERS

Of the roughly 69,000 announcers working in the United States, nearly 60 percent work in broadcast media. Some work on a freelance basis on individual assignments for networks, stations, advertising agencies, and other producers of commercials. About 30 percent of announcers work part time.

Some companies own several television or radio stations; some belong to networks such as ABC, CBS, NBC, or Fox, while others are independent. While radio and television stations are located throughout the United States, major markets where better-paying jobs are found are generally near large metropolitan areas.

STARTING OUT

One way to enter this field is to apply for an entry-level job rather than an announcer position. It is also advisable to start at a small station. Most announcers start in jobs such as production secretary, production assistant, researcher, or reporter in small stations. As opportunities arise, it is common for announcers to move from one job to another. You may be able to find work as a disc jockey, sportscaster, or news reporter. Network jobs are few, and the competition for them is great. You must have several years of experience as well as a college education to be considered for these positions.

You must audition before you will be employed as an announcer. You should carefully select audition material to show a prospective employer the full range of your abilities. In addition to presenting prepared materials, you may be asked to read material that you have not seen previously, such as a commercial, news release, dramatic selection, or poem.

ADVANCEMENT

Most successful announcers advance from small stations to large ones. Experienced announcers usually have held several jobs. The most successful announcers may be those who work for the networks. Usually, because of network locations, announcers must live in or near the country's largest cities.

Some careers lead from announcing to other aspects of radio or television work. More people are employed in sales, promotion, and planning than in performing; often they are paid more than announcers. Because the networks employ relatively few announcers in proportion to the rest of the broadcasting professionals, a candidate must have several years of experience and specific background in several news areas before being considered for an audition. Top announcers generally are college graduates.

EARNINGS

Salaries for announcers vary widely, but generally they are low. The exceptions are those announcers who work for major networks and stations that serve large metropolitan areas.

The U.S. Department of Labor reports that median hourly earnings for radio and television announcers were $10.97 in 2004, which is about $22,820 a year. The lowest-paid 10 percent made less than $6.22 an hour ($12,940 a year) and the highest-paid 10 percent made more than $28.29 an hour ($58,830 a year).

Nationally known announcers and newscasters who appear regularly on network television programs receive salaries that may be quite impressive—sometimes more than $1 million a year. For those who become top television personalities in large metropolitan areas, salaries also are quite rewarding.

Most radio or television stations broadcast 24 hours a day. Although much of the material may be prerecorded, announcing staff must often be available and as a result may work considerable overtime or split shifts, especially in smaller stations. Evening, night, weekend, and holiday duty may provide additional compensation.

WORK ENVIRONMENT

Work in radio and television stations is usually very pleasant. Almost all stations are housed in modern facilities. The maintenance of technical electronic equipment requires temperature and dust control, and people who work around such equipment benefit from the precautions taken to preserve it.

Announcers' jobs may provide opportunities to meet well-known or celebrity persons. Being at the center of an important communications medium can make the broadcaster more keenly aware of current issues and divergent points of view than the average person.

Announcers and newscasters usually work a 40-hour week, but they may work irregular hours. They may report for work at a very early hour in the morning or work late into the night. Some radio stations operate on a 24-hour basis. All-night announcers may be alone in the station during their working hours.

OUTLOOK

Competition for entry-level employment in announcing during the coming years is expected to be keen, as the broadcasting industry always attracts more applicants than are needed to fill available openings. There is a better chance of working in radio than in television because there are more radio stations—as well as new opportunities with the emergence of satellite radio. Local television stations usually carry a high percentage of network programs and need only a very small staff to carry out local operations.

The U.S. Department of Labor predicts that opportunities for announcers will decline through 2014 due to the slowing growth of new radio and television stations. Openings will result mainly from those who leave the industry or the labor force. The trend among major networks, and to some extent among many smaller radio and TV stations, is toward specialization in such fields as sportscasting or weather forecasting. Newscasters who specialize in such areas as business, consumer, and health news should have an advantage over other job applicants.

FOR MORE INFORMATION

For a list of schools offering degrees in broadcasting as well as scholarship information, contact
Broadcast Education Association
1771 N Street, NW
Washington, DC 20036-2891
Tel: 888-380-7222
Email: beainfo@beaweb.org
http://www.beaweb.org

For broadcast education, support, and scholarship information, contact
National Association of Broadcasters
1771 N Street, NW
Washington, DC 20036-2891
Tel: 202-429-5300
Email: nab@nab.org
http://www.nab.org

For information on union membership, contact
National Association of Broadcast Employees and Technicians
Email: nabet@nabetcwa.org
http://nabetcwa.org

For general information, contact
National Association of Farm Broadcasters
PO Box 500
Platte City, MO 64079-0500
Tel: 816-431-4032
Email: info@nafb.com
http://nafb.com

For a booklet on careers in cable, contact
National Cable and Telecommunications Association
25 Massachusetts Avenue, NW
Washington, DC 20001-1430
Tel: 202-222-2300
http://www.ncta.com

For scholarship and internship information, contact
Radio-Television News Directors Association
Radio-Television News Directors Foundation
1600 K Street, NW, Suite 700
Washington, DC 20006-2838
Tel: 202-659-6510
Email: rtnda@rtnda.org
http://www.rtnda.org

Radio and Television Program Directors

OVERVIEW

Radio and television program directors plan and schedule program material for stations and networks. They determine the entertainment programs, news broadcasts, and other program material their organizations offer to the public. At a large network, the program director may supervise a large programming staff. At a small station, one person may manage the station and also handle all programming duties.

HISTORY

Radio broadcasting in the United States began after World War I. The first commercial radio station, KDKA in Pittsburgh, came on the air in 1920 with a broadcast of presidential election returns. About a dozen radio stations were broadcasting by 1921. In 1926 the first national network linked stations across the country. According to the *CIA World Factbook*, there were 4,789 AM and 8,961 FM stations broadcasting in the United States in 2006.

The first public demonstration of television in the United States came in 1939 at the opening of the New York World's Fair. Further development was limited during World War II, but by 1953 there were about 120 stations. According to the *CIA World Factbook*, there were 2,218 television broadcast stations in the United States in 2006. The National Cable and Telecommunications Association reports that between 2002 and 2005, the number of cable networks nearly doubled, from 287 to 531 channels.

THE JOB

Program directors plan and schedule program material for radio and television stations and networks. They work in both commercial and public broadcasting and may be employed by individual radio or television stations, regional or national networks, or cable television systems.

The material program directors work with includes entertainment programs, public service programs, newscasts, sportscasts, and commercial announcements. Program directors decide what material is broadcast and when it is scheduled; they work with other staff members to develop programs and buy programs from independent producers. They are guided by such factors as the budget available for program material, the audience their station or network seeks to attract, their organization's policies on content and other matters, and the kinds of products advertised in the various commercial announcements.

In addition, program directors may set up schedules for the program staff, audition and hire announcers and other on-the-air personnel, and assist the sales department in negotiating contracts with sponsors of commercial announcements. The duties of individual program directors are determined by such factors as whether they work in radio or television, for a small or large organization, for one station or a network, or in a commercial or public operation.

At small radio stations the owner or manager may be responsible for programming, but at larger radio stations and at television stations the staff usually includes a program director. At medium to large radio and television stations the program director usually has a staff that includes such personnel as music librarians, music directors, editors for tape or film segments, and writers. Some stations and networks employ *public service directors*. It is the responsibility of these individuals to plan and schedule radio or television public service programs and announcements in such fields as education, religion, and civic and government affairs. Networks often employ *broadcast operations directors,* who coordinate the activities of the personnel who prepare network program schedules, review program schedules, issue daily corrections, and advise affiliated stations on their schedules.

Program directors must carefully coordinate the various elements for a station while keeping in tune with the listeners, viewers, advertisers, and sponsors.

Other managers in radio and television broadcasting include production managers, operations directors, news directors, and sports directors. The work of program directors usually does not include the duties of *radio directors* or *television directors,* who direct rehearsals and integrate all the elements of a performance.

REQUIREMENTS

High School

If you are interested in this career, you should take courses that develop your communication skills in high school. Such classes include English, debate, and speech. You also should take business courses to develop your management skills; current events and history courses to develop your understanding of the news and the trends that affect the public's interests; and such courses as dance, drama, music, and painting to expand your understanding of the creative arts. Finally, don't neglect your computer skills. You will probably use computers throughout your career to file reports, maintain schedules, and plan future programming projects.

Postsecondary Training

Those with the most thorough educational backgrounds will find it easiest to advance in this field. A college degree, therefore, is recommended for this field. Possible majors for those interested in this work include radio and television production and broadcasting, communications, liberal arts, or business administration. You will probably take English, economics, business administration, computer, and media classes. You may also wish to acquire some technical training that will help you understand the engineering aspects of broadcasting.

Other Requirements

Program directors must be creative, alert, and adaptable people who stay up to date on the public's interests and attitudes and are able to recognize the potential in new ideas. They must be able to work under pressure and be willing to work long hours, and they must be able to work with all kinds of people. Program directors also must be good managers who can make decisions, oversee costs and deadlines, and attend to details.

EXPLORING

If your high school or college has a radio or television station, you should volunteer to work on the staff. You also should look for part-time or summer jobs at local radio or television stations. You may not be able to plan the programming at a local station, but you will see how a station works and be able to make contacts with those in the field. If you can't find a job at a local station, at least arrange for a visit and ask to talk to the personnel. You may be able to "shadow" a program director for a day—that is, follow that director for the workday and see what his or her job entails.

EMPLOYERS

According to the *CIA World Factbook,* there were 2,218 broadcast television stations and 13,750 radio stations in the United States in 2006. Cable television stations add another option for employment.

Large conglomerates own some stations, while others are owned individually. While radio and television stations are located all over the country, the largest stations with the highest paid positions are located in large metropolitan areas.

STARTING OUT

Program director jobs are not entry-level positions. A degree and extensive experience in the field is required. Most program directors have technical and on-air experience in either radio or television. While you are in college you should investigate the availability of internships, since internships are almost essential for prospective job candidates. Your college career services office should also have information on job openings. Private and state employment agencies may also prove useful resources. You can also send resumes to radio and television stations or apply in person.

Beginners should be willing to relocate, as they are unlikely to find employment in large cities. They usually start at small stations with fewer employees, allowing them a chance to learn a variety of skills.

ADVANCEMENT

Most beginners start in entry-level jobs and work several years before they have enough experience to become program directors. Experienced program directors usually advance by moving from small stations to larger stations and networks or by becoming station managers.

EARNINGS

Salaries for radio and television program directors vary widely based on such factors as size and location of the station, whether the station is commercial or public, and experience of the director. Television program directors generally earn more than their counterparts in radio. According to the U.S. Department of Labor, median annual earnings of general and operations managers in radio and television broadcasting were $88,878 in 2004.

According to a salary survey by the Radio-Television News Directors Association, radio news directors earned a median of $30,500, and salaries ranged from a low of $10,000 to a high of $72,000 in 2001. Television news directors earned a median of $64,000, with salaries ranging from $18,000 to $250,000.

Both radio and television program directors usually receive health and life coverage benefits and sometimes yearly bonuses as well.

WORK ENVIRONMENT

Program directors at small stations often work 44 to 48 hours a week and frequently work evenings, late at night, and weekends. At larger stations, which have more personnel, program directors usually work 40-hour weeks.

Program directors frequently work under pressure because of the need to maintain precise timing and meet the needs of sponsors, performers, and other staff members.

Although the work is sometimes stressful and demanding, program directors usually work in pleasant environments with creative staffs. They also interact with the community to arrange programming and deal with a variety of people.

OUTLOOK

All radio and television stations, cable television systems, and regional and national networks employ program directors or have other employees whose duties include programming. According to the U.S. Department of Labor, employment in broadcasting is expected to increase 11 percent over the 2004–14 period, slower than the average of 14 percent growth for all industries combined. This slow growth rate is attributed to industry consolidation, introduction of new technologies, greater use of prepared programming, and competition from other media.

Competition for radio and television program director jobs is strong. There are more opportunities for beginners in radio than there are in television. Most radio and television stations in large cities hire only experienced workers.

New radio (including those created by the emergence of satellite radio) and television stations and new cable television systems are expected to create additional openings for program directors, but some radio stations are eliminating program director positions by installing automatic programming equipment or combining those responsibilities with other positions.

FOR MORE INFORMATION

For a list of schools offering degrees in broadcasting, contact
Broadcast Education Association
1771 N Street, NW
Washington, DC 20036-2891
Tel: 888-380-7222
Email: beainfo@beaweb.org
http://www.beaweb.org

For broadcast education, support, and scholarship information, contact
National Association of Broadcasters
1771 N Street, NW
Washington, DC 20036-2891
Tel: 202-429-5300
Email: nab@nab.org
http://www.nab.org

For information on student membership, contact
National Association of Farm Broadcasters
PO Box 500
Platte City, MO 64079-0500
Tel: 816-431-4032
http://nafb.com

For a booklet on careers in cable, contact
National Cable and Telecommunications Association
1724 Massachusetts Avenue, NW
Washington, DC 20036-1903
Tel: 202-775-3550
http://www.ncta.com

For scholarship and internship information, contact
Radio-Television News Directors Association
1600 K Street, NW, Suite 700
Washington, DC 20006-2838
Tel: 202-659-6510
Email: rtnda@rtnda.org
http://www.rtnda.org

Radio Producers

OVERVIEW

Radio producers plan, rehearse, and produce live or recorded programs. They work with the music, on-air personalities, sound effects, and technology to put together an entire radio show. They schedule interviews and arrange for promotional events.

According to the *CIA World Factbook*, Federal Communications Commission (FCC), the United States alone has 13,750 radio stations. Larger stations employ radio producers, while smaller stations may combine those duties with those of the program director or disc jockey. While most radio producers work at radio stations, some work to produce a particular show and then sell that show to various stations.

HISTORY

As long as radio has existed, people have been behind the scenes to make sure that what the audience hears is what the station wants them to hear. A wide variety of administrative, programming, and technical people work behind the scenes of radio shows to create a professional broadcast.

Scheduled broadcasting began with a program broadcast by radio station KDKA in Pittsburgh. By 1923, 2.5 million radios had been sold. In the 1930s, radio personalities were household names, and even then, numerous people worked behind the scenes, arranging interviews and coordinating production.

Before television, radio producers would direct the on-air soap operas as well as the news, weather, and music. With the added technology of today's radio broadcast, radio producers are even more

School Subjects
English
Journalism
Speech

Personal Skills
Communication/ideas
Leadership/management

Work Environment
Primarily indoors
Primarily one location

Minimum Education Level
Bachelor's degree

Salary Range
$26,940 to $55,400 to
$84,190+

Certification or Licensing
None available

Outlook
More slowly than the
average

DOT
159

GOE
01.03.01

NOC
5131

O*NET-SOC
27-2012.00

important in mixing the special effects, locations, personalities, and formats in ways that create a good radio show.

The Internet has made the radio producer's job easier in some ways and more challenging in others. Web sites specifically for producers provide a community where ideas can be exchanged for shows, news, jokes, and more. However, with the new frontier of broadcasting on the Internet, radio producers have one more duty to add to their long list of responsibilities.

THE JOB

The identity and style of a radio program is a result of the collaborations of on-air and off-air professionals. Radio disc jockeys talk the talk during a broadcast, and producers walk the walk behind the scenes. But in many situations, particularly with smaller radio stations, the disc jockey is also the show's producer.

Also, many show producers have disc jockey experience. This experience, combined with technical expertise, helps producers effectively plan their shows.

Brent Lee, a radio producer for WFMS, a country radio station in Indianapolis, began his career while still in high school at the small radio station in his home town. This early on-air experience, combined with his degree in telecommunications and political science from Ball State University, helped to give Lee the necessary background for his current position.

Radio producers rely on the public's very particular tastes—differences in taste allow for many different kinds of radio to exist, to serve many different segments of a community. In developing radio programs, producers take into consideration the marketplace—they listen to other area radio stations and determine what's needed and appreciated in the community, and what there may already be too much of. They conduct surveys and interviews to find out what the public wants to hear. They decide which age groups they want to pursue and develop a format based on what appeals to these listeners. These efforts result in a station's identity, which is very important. Listeners associate a station with the kind of music it plays, how much music it plays, the type of news and conversation presented, and the station's on-air personalities.

Based on this feedback, and on market research, radio disc jockeys/producers devise music playlists and music libraries. They each develop an individual on-air identity, or personality, and they invite guests who will interest their listeners. Keeping a show running on time is also the responsibility of a producer. This involves carefully weaving many different elements into a show, including music, news reports, traffic reports, and interviews.

As the producer of the "Jim, Kevin, and Bill Show," Lee arrives at the station at about 4:15 A.M. each morning to prep for the morning show. The show broadcasts from 5:00 A.M. to 9:00 A.M. each morning and considers its main audience to be the "morning drivers" on their way to work or school.

The time of the broadcast is one key to planning a radio show. Because of the typical listeners of the morning show, traffic reports are given every 10 minutes. These reports are mixed with weather, news, and music. Although the rest of the day, WFMS listeners will hear 13 songs each hour, the morning show typically plays between six and eight songs per hour. Those songs are interspersed with six traffic reports, four weather forecasts, a variety of national, local, and entertainment news, and the typical morning disc jockey banter.

The audience of the country music radio station is mostly female, and the morning show is billed as "good, clean fun" by the station, promoting the family nature of the program.

In addition to keeping in touch with the listening public, producers keep track of current events. They consult newspapers and other radio programs to determine what subjects to discuss on their morning shows. One of the newest tools that Lee uses is a Web site designed specifically for morning shows. The site provides a forum to share ideas and ask questions.

"There are a couple of things each day that can be used," says Lee. "Since we're a family show, we have to throw some of it out, but it's a really good resource."

Radio producers write copy for and coordinate on-air commercials, which are usually recorded in advance. They also devise contests, from large public events to small, on-air trivia competitions.

Though a majority of radio stations have music formats, radio producers also work for 24-hour news stations, public broadcasting, and talk radio. Producing news programs and radio documentaries involves a great deal of research, booking guests, writing scripts, and interviewing.

"One of the most attractive qualities about this job is it's fun," says Lee. "Each day, I spend half of my first five hours laughing."

REQUIREMENTS

High School

Writing skills are valuable in any profession but especially in radio. Take composition and literature courses and other courses that require essays and term papers. Journalism courses will not only help you develop your writing skills, but they will teach you about the nature and history of media. You'll learn about deadlines and how to put a complete project (such as a newspaper or yearbook) together. Speech courses are also necessary if you plan on getting on-air experience or managing other workers.

Business courses and clubs frequently require students to put together projects; starting any business is similar to producing your own radio show. Use such a project as an opportunity to become familiar with the market research, interviewing, and writing that are all part of a radio producer's job. For both the future radio producer and the future disc jockey, a theater department offers great learning opportunities. Drama or theater classes, which are frequently involved in productions, may provide opportunities for learning about funding, advertising, casting, and other fundamentals similar to a radio production.

If your school has a radio station, get involved with it in any way you can. Check with your local radio stations; some may offer part-time jobs to high school students interested in becoming producers and disc jockeys.

Postsecondary Training

Most journalism and communications schools at universities offer programs in broadcasting. Radio producers and announcers often start their training in journalism schools, and they receive hands-on instruction at campus radio stations. These broadcasting programs are generally news-centered, providing great opportunities for students interested in producing news programs, daily newscasts, and documentaries. News directors and program managers of radio stations generally want to hire people who have a good, well-rounded education with a foundation of history, geography, political science, and literature.

Other Requirements

In order to be a successful radio producer, you should be well versed in the English language (or the language you broadcast in) and be a creative thinker who can combine several elements into one project. The ability to understand technical equipment and coordinate it with on-air events is also necessary.

A healthy curiosity about people and the world will help radio producers find new topics for news shows, new guests for call-ins, and new ideas for music formats. There are no physical requirements to be a radio producer, although those starting as disc jockeys need a strong, clear voice to be heard over the airwaves.

EXPLORING

Getting your feet wet early is a good idea for all radio careers. Small radio stations are often willing to let young, inexperienced people work either behind-the-scenes or on-air. Getting a job or an internship at one of the small stations in your area may be as simple as asking for one.

Many high schools and universities have on-site radio stations where students can get hands-on experience at all different levels. As you explore the career further, you might want to interview a radio producer to make sure that the job requirements and description are still of interest to you.

Since most people don't start out as a producer, experience in any area of radio is helpful, so talk to local disc jockeys or program directors as well.

EMPLOYERS

There has been a steady growth in the number of radio stations in the United States. According to the *CIA World Factbook*, there were 13,750 radio stations as of 2006. Many stations combine the position of radio producer with that of the disc jockey or program director, so depending on the size of the station and market, producers may or may not be able to find a suitable employer.

Due to the Telecommunications Act of 1996, companies can own an unlimited number of radio stations nationwide with an eight-station limit within one market area, depending on the size of the market. When this legislation took effect, mergers and acquisitions changed the face of the radio industry. So while the pool of employers is smaller, the number of stations continues to rise.

STARTING OUT

Radio producers usually start work at radio stations in any capacity possible. After working for a while in a part-time position gaining experience and making connections, a young, dedicated producer will find opportunities to work in production or on air.

Both experience and a college education are generally needed to become a radio producer. It is best if both the experience and the education are well rounded with exposure to on-air and off-air positions as well as a good working knowledge of the world in which we live.

Although some future producers begin their first radio jobs in paid positions, many serve unpaid internships or volunteer to help run their college or high school station. Even if this entry-level work is unpaid, the experience gained is one of the key necessities to furthering a career in any type of radio work.

With experience as a disc jockey or behind-the-scenes person, an aspiring radio producer might try to land a position at another station, most likely within a station and format they are used to.

ADVANCEMENT

Radio producers are a key link in putting together a radio show. Once they have experience coordinating all the elements that go into a radio production, it is possible to move into a program director position or, possibly in the future, to general manager.

Another way to advance is to move from being the producer of a small show to a larger one, or move from a small station to a larger one. Some producers move into the freelance arena, producing their own shows that they sell to several radio stations.

EARNINGS

According to the U.S. Department of Labor, producers employed in all fields (including radio) earned salaries that ranged from less than $26,940 to more than $84,190 in 2004. Producers employed in radio and television broadcasting earned mean annual salaries of $55,400 in 2004. Like many radio jobs, there is a wide salary range resulting from differences in market size and station size of each radio station. Salaries for radio producers have been relatively flat, according to the Radio and Television News Directors Association, with little growth over the previous few years.

Most large stations offer full-time employees typical benefits, including health and life insurance.

WORK ENVIRONMENT

Radio producers generally work indoors in a busy environment, although some location and outdoor work might be required. The atmosphere at a radio station is generally very pleasant; however, smaller stations may not be modern, with much of the investment going into high-tech equipment for the broadcasts.

Full-time radio producers usually work more than 40 hours per week planning, scheduling, and producing radio shows. Also, according to the schedule of their shows, early morning, late night, or weekend work might be required. Radio is a 24-hour-a-day, seven-day-a-week production, requiring constant staffing.

Producers work with disc jockeys and program directors in planning radio shows, and they also work with advertising personnel to produce radio commercials. In addition to this collaboration, they may work alone doing research for the show. Working with the public is another aspect of the radio producer's job. Promotions and events may require contact with businesspeople and listeners.

OUTLOOK

The U.S. Department of Labor predicts slower-than-average employment growth in the radio industry through 2014. In the past, radio station ownership was highly regulated by the government, limiting the number of stations a person or company could own. Recent deregulation has made multiple-station ownership and consolidation of offices possible. Radio stations now are bought and sold at a more rapid pace. This may result in a radio station changing formats as well as entire staffs. Though some radio producers are able to stay at a station over a period of several years, people going into radio should be prepared to change employers at some point in their careers.

Another trend that is affecting radio producing jobs is the increasing use of programming created by services outside the broadcasting industry. Satellite radio, in which subscribers pay a monthly fee for access to more than 100 radio stations, will be a big threat to smaller, marginal stations.

Competition is stiff for all radio jobs. Graduates of college broadcasting programs are finding a scarcity of work in media. Paid internships will also be difficult to find—many students of radio will have to work for free for a while to gain experience. Radio producers may find more opportunities as freelancers, developing their own programs independently and selling them to stations.

FOR MORE INFORMATION

For a list of schools offering degrees in broadcasting as well as scholarship information, contact
Broadcast Education Association
1771 N Street, NW
Washington, DC 20036-2891
Tel: 888-380-7222
Email: beainfo@beaweb.org
http://www.beaweb.org

The FCC offers information on media guidelines, including all radio laws. For more information, contact
Federal Communications Commission (FCC)
445 12th Street, SW
Washington, DC 20554-0001

Tel: 888-225-5322
Email: fccinfo@fcc.gov
http://www.fcc.gov

For college programs and union information, contact
National Association of Broadcast Employees and Technicians
Email: nabet@nabetcwa.org
http://nabetcwa.org

For broadcast education, support, and scholarship information, contact
National Association of Broadcasters
1771 N Street, NW
Washington, DC 20036-2891
Tel: 202-429-5300
Email: nab@nab.org
http://www.nab.org

For scholarship and internship information, contact
Radio-Television News Directors Association
1600 K Street, NW, Suite 700
Washington, DC 20006-2838
Tel: 202-659-6510
Email: rtnda@rtnda.org
http://www.rtnda.org

INTERVIEW

Sue Kopen Katcef is a lecturer/executive producer at the University of Maryland's Philip Merrill College of Journalism/UMTV in College Park, Maryland. She discussed her career and the education of broadcast journalism students with the editors of Careers in Focus: Broadcasting.

Q. Tell us about your work at the university.

A. I am currently a lecturer/executive producer for the Philip Merrill College of Journalism. I am the only teacher of the first broadcast news writing/radio production class our broadcast majors are required to take. On occasion, I am called on to teach other classes as well. But, my other "primary" responsibility is to serve as the executive producer for our nightly student TV show, the award-winning *Maryland Newsline* that's produced by an advanced broadcast news reporting class, which is comprised of both graduate and undergraduate students. This is a regional newscast, with a heavy emphasis on public affairs reporting. Students/reporters cover stories all over the state during their semester. Because of my many years of covering Maryland news and politics, I am often a resource for reporters on where to go and with whom to speak—in addition to providing perspective for their stories. So, I frequently help with assignments and provide guidance for scripts. In addition, I oversee the entire newscast and am the instructor who supervises and guides the students from our producing class who use the nightly newscast as their lab. That role involves setting the nightly rundown in place, editing stories written by the producers, providing feedback, and supervising them as the show takes place. On occasion, I am pressed into service to help as a crew member—with the Teleprompter, computer generated graphics (the names/descriptions/location/titles that appear under someone in a news story), or even fill in as the nightly producer.

One other duty I have is to oversee the weekly production of a radio news program, "Terp Weekly Edition," which airs on the campus FM radio station. It is largely the work of the students from my news writing/reporting class, but also involves some former students with a smattering of volunteers. I appoint the executive producer (always a former student) and the production manager (who's also already taken the class). This is a public-radio style, long-form format (average package runs about 1:30) that's recorded on Fridays and airs several times the following week. I work closely with the executives of the show, help with story ideas, and review the weekly script and final product. Students from my class are required to take turns serving as weekly "on call" reporters according to a schedule I set up. In addition, they can gain extra credit for providing packages for the show and anchoring.

I also maintain my working relationship with WBAL Radio. I periodically fill in as an anchor or cover a story. I do it as much for the opportunity to stay in touch with the developing/changing technology (and my personal peace of mind) as I do to maintain the respect of the students I'm teaching. I am also active in a couple of professional associations (the Society of Professional Journalists and the Radio and Television News Directors Association) and belong to several others in order to stay in touch with what's happening in the industry and to maintain my contacts. They are relationships that often pay off for my students.

Q. Tell us about the student television newsroom at UMTV.

A. There are at least five classes that operate out of the UMTV newsroom (field/studio TV production class; TV reporting class—which is next in the broadcast sequence following my class; documentary class; advanced TV reporting class—Capital News Service Broadcast Bureau; and our TV producing class). It is a combined newsroom/studio. We have six edit bays—all Avid non-linear. We also have linear facilities, but they are not in the studio. We have a fully functioning assignment desk. In 2006, a new, custom-made news set was introduced, which gives our student TV newscasts their own unique look. It's a giant step forward for our productions. We have approximately eight PCs on which the AP's ENPS (Electronic News Production System) is installed. ENPS is where we create the nightly rundown—students write their packages/scripts, etc. All student shows use students as crew, and we always rely on volunteers for our nightly show to fill out those slots. Our advanced broadcast reporting class is currently capped at 10 members; often, we have fewer—so with two anchors, plus the necessary tech jobs to fill, we are ALWAYS in need of extras to get the show on the air, but we always manage to pull it off. Programming from UMTV, including our nightly newscast, airs on cable systems in the suburban Maryland counties of Montgomery and Prince George's (just outside Washington, D.C.) and Baltimore City. This is GREAT exposure for our students.

Q. What are the most important personal and professional qualities for broadcast journalism majors?

A. Unquestionably: passion, curiosity, the ability to think on their feet and think critically and write (and speak) well and effectively. They should be able to remain cool under fire and be able to find other open doors when one is closed on them while pursuing a story. And, they need to stick to the principles of good ethical behavior.

Q. What advice would you provide to high school students interested in careers in broadcast journalism?

A. Just do it and write, write, write. Work for the newspaper or yearbook. If your school has some kind of broadcast outlet, get involved. If there's an opportunity to work for a local paper or TV or radio station, do that, too. Students may be surprised at the number of media outlets that welcome high school students as interns. But, they can't be shy. They MUST go after it. And be a news CONSUMER! Don't say you want to enter the news business and not be aware of what's going on around you. Read, listen, and watch as much as you possibly can. And that includes OPPOSING viewpoints.

Q. What advice would you give to broadcast journalism students as they seek to enter the field?

A. Get as many internships as you can and network at every opportunity. Join professional associations: the Radio-Television News Directors Association and the Society of Professional Journalists, just to name two. There are certainly many others.

Real-Time Captioners

OVERVIEW

Real-time captioners operate a computer-aided transcription (CAT) stenotype system to create closed captions for use in live television broadcasts, in classroom instruction, or in other scenarios requiring live translating or interpreting on the computer. Computer-Aided Real-time Translation (CART) refers to use of machine steno shorthand skills to produce real-time text on a computer. Generally, captioning systems use a modified stenotype machine connected to a computer. The real-time captioner inputs the captions phonetically (transcription or speech sounds) on the steno machine, and the sounds are then translated into English words by the computer using a special dictionary created by the captioner. During a live broadcast, the captions are entered as the program progresses, much as a court reporter transcribes a trial as it progresses. The input data is sent along telephone lines to the broadcast point, where the caption codes become part of the television signal.

HISTORY

Real-time captioning technology arose from a need to make live broadcasts accessible to deaf and hard-of-hearing people. To meet this need, the National Captioning Institute (NCI), founded in 1979, became the chief architect of the computer-based technology needed to bring captions to real-time audiences nationwide. At first, the NCI provided captions only for prerecorded programs. Captions were prepared in advance by people who were not court reporters. It soon became apparent, however, that captions were needed for live

QUICK FACTS

School Subjects
English
Government

Personal Skills
Communication/ideas
Following instructions

Work Environment
Primarily indoors
Primarily one location

Minimum Education Level
Bachelor's degree

Salary Range
$23,730 to $42,720 to
  $78,840+

Certification or Licensing
Recommended

Outlook
Faster than the average

DOT
203

GOE
07.05.03

NOC
N/A

O*NET-SOC
N/A

television, so the NCI went to work developing a system that could prepare captions for live broadcast.

The NCI introduced real-time captioning to eager audiences in April 1982 when it captioned the Academy Awards. Today, real-time captioners create captions for a wide range of live broadcasts on network, cable, syndication, and pay-per-view services. All programs on prime-time schedules of the four major commercial networks are now captioned, many by real-time captioners.

Real-time captions are generated within seconds after a word is spoken. They are made possible by highly skilled court reporters who receive months of specialized retraining to become first-class real-time captioners.

THE JOB

The refined skills of real-time captioners are called upon every day to bring the latest news, sports, and entertainment to a diverse group consisting not only of the deaf and hard-of-hearing but young children learning to read and those learning English as a second language. Although captioning a live program, meeting, or other event may seem rather straightforward on the surface, a great deal of work, anxiety, and preparation goes into ensuring that the words appearing on screen come out as smoothly and effortlessly as possible. Real-time captioning requires much dexterity and discipline to be able to reach the higher speeds required—250 words a minute—and good brain-to-hand coordination to get it all down quickly *and* accurately.

There is also much preparation that must be done by real-time captioners before they can caption a live television broadcast. It takes about one and a half to two hours to prepare for an average news broadcast, using preparation materials obtained from the broadcaster and the captioner's own research. (Special broadcasts such as holiday parades, the Super Bowl, or the Olympics can take days or even weeks of preparation.) Captioners call this preshow preparation *dictionary-building*.

Captioners working for established captioning houses will usually have access to all types of reference materials—everything from *Star Stats Who's Who in Hollywood* to the *Congressional Staff Directory*. Captioners working on their own will want to think about what kinds of materials to include in their own libraries.

Real-time captioners prepare for a job by going through resource materials to find words that might come up during a broadcast and then develop steno codes that they use to "write" these words when they do come up. It is important that captioners test all the briefs developed for complicated names to make sure they are translating properly. Because captioners will hear names and words during the broadcast that they have not prepared dictionary entries for, they must learn to "write around" the actual words and listen for titles. In this way, captioners can write "The former Secretary of State" instead of "Henry Kissinger," for example.

While striving to keep errors to a minimum, captioners will occasionally make mistakes that go out over the air. For example, in real-time captioning, the phrase "Olympic tryouts," which would require the captioner to type five key strokes on a stenotype machine, might come out (and actually did) as "old limp pig tryouts" if strokes are entered that the computer cannot match correctly.

CART reporters also work in classroom settings, where they might be seen with a notebook computer and steno keyboard, sitting next to a deaf person. CART reporters write down everything that happens, making sure the notebook computer screen is turned so the deaf person can see it. To help the client better understand what is going on, they may paraphrase or interpret the proceedings, not just create a verbatim record, as in a courtroom. Real-time reporters can also cover meetings, with captions shown on large projection screens. Additionally, computer technology allows highly skilled court reporters to provide real-time captioning in the courtroom, which has great value for large numbers of deaf or hard-of-hearing judges, attorneys, and litigants or those who have difficulty understanding English. Also, judges and attorneys can scroll back to earlier statements during the trial and mark text for later reference.

One major difference between real-time captioning for television broadcast and other live-display settings and verbatim reporting, as is frequently done in courtrooms and lawyers' offices, is that captioning's main purpose is to let the viewer who is deaf or hard of hearing understand the story being told on the screen. It is not enough to listen only for the phonetic strokes; the real-time captioner must also listen for context.

Sheri Smargon works for a captioning company in Tampa, Florida. "I caption the news for about 12 different stations around the country," she says. "My company has more, but I have regular cities that I'm usually responsible for. The news consists of anything from a half-hour program to two hours of straight news. I also caption NBA and MLB games." While captioning, Smargon doesn't receive a TV picture. "I get an audio feed only, so I just write what I hear," she says. "Hockey games were the hardest . . . everyone's name sounds alike!"

Before beginning even limited on-air captioning, captioner trainees must spend at least three to six months in training, eight hours a day, five days a week, and up to one year of real-time captioning before doing certain specialized programming. As a vital part of the production team, captioners must also become intimately familiar with the programs they are captioning to know what to expect and to anticipate the unexpected.

A typical day for a captioner trainee would include preparing for a practice broadcast by creating a job dictionary, then writing that practice broadcast for supervisors, who would make suggestions as to conflict resolution, editing, brief form, style, and format. Later, the trainee would review the broadcast and make the necessary dictionary entries. Trainees would sit in on a variety of broadcasts with more experienced captioners.

Real-time captioning for television is generally performed in a production control room, equipped with several television sets and networked computer systems, giving the environment a high-tech look and feel. Sometimes, one captioner will write a show alone; sometimes two captioners will share a show, depending on whether there are commercials or not. No captioner can maintain a high accuracy level without taking regular breaks. On a show with no commercials, two captioners would typically switch back and forth about every 10 minutes.

As a show gets closer to air, the environment in the control room becomes tense, as the real-time captioner scrambles to get last-minute information in the computer. Then a deep breath, and the countdown begins . . . "Good evening, I'm Brian Williams."

The captioner strokes the steno keys while listening to the live broadcast, transcribing the broadcast accurately while inserting correct punctuation and other symbols. (Double arrows at the beginning of a sentence indicate that a new speaker is speaking.) Those strokes are converted to electronic impulses, which travel through a cable to the computer. The steno strokes are matched with the correct entries on the captioner's personal dictionary. That data is then sent electronically to the broadcast site, where it gets added to the broadcaster's video signal. Within two to three seconds, people across the country can see those captions—if they have televisions with a built-in decoder chip or a set with a decoder connected to it.

Some kinds of captioning can be done from home, mainly broadcasts for local television stations. The equipment needed (which may be provided by the employer) includes a computer, an Internet connection hardware and software, a steno machine, and other appropriate software. Captioners may even choose to work for companies that specialize in producing captions remotely, with just an audio feed, thereby allowing more home-based operations. Getting started in the business, however, usually requires an on-site presence until confidence and trust are established. Obviously, live events that are not broadcast will require a real-time captioner on site.

REQUIREMENTS

High School
You should take typing and computer courses to increase keyboard speed and accuracy and to develop an understanding of word processing programs. Because you'll be working with a variety of news, sports, and entertainment programs, you should keep up on current events by taking journalism, social studies, and government courses. English composition and speech classes can help you develop your vocabulary and grammar skills.

Postsecondary Training
You should first complete training to become a court and conference reporter (stenographer), which takes anywhere from two to four years. An associate's or bachelor's degree in court and conference reporting, or satisfactory completion of other two-year equivalent programs, is usually required. Because of the additional training needed to learn computer and English grammar skills, some two-year programs have become three-year programs. In fact, many real-time reporters and their employers believe that additional formal education in the arts and sciences is needed to perform the work properly and to adapt to the swift technological changes taking place. They are urging the National Court Reporters Association (NCRA), to which most captioners and other reporters belong, to require a bachelor's degree for entry into the court reporting profession, which would extend to captioning as well. A few four-year college programs already exist, to allow students a well-rounded background. A degree in English (or the primary language in which captioning will be done) or linguistics would be helpful. Others argue, however, that while a formal education is beneficial, many court reporters who never earned a four-year degree are working successfully with high skill levels.

Even after graduating from court reporting school, you will have to undergo more specialized training, during which you'll hone your reporting skills to achieve the proficiency needed to create broadcast-quality captions.

Certification or Licensing

Typically, the reporter considering real-time captioning work has passed the Registered Professional Reporter (RPR) exam given by the NCRA or a comparable state certification exam. Potential employers may even require it. The skills and knowledge needed to pass this exam are similar to those required for captioning, though not as stringent. Anyone capable of doing broadcast-quality captioning work can easily get RPR certification. Court reporters may also earn certifications awarded by the American Association of Electronic Reporters and Transcribers and the Verbatim Reporters Association. Contact these organizations for more information.

Other Requirements

You should have extreme proficiency in machine-shorthand skills and an ability to perform under pressure. Familiarity with CAT systems is usually preferred, as is previous court or field reporting experience. It generally takes several years of court reporting experience to be able to take and transcribe complex testimony with the high levels of speed and accuracy that real-time captioning demands.

Real-time captioners must also possess an incredible amount of concentration. Besides typing accurately at speeds of 200 to 250 words a minute to keep up with the fastest natural speakers, they must also anticipate commercial breaks so as not to cut off captions in midsentence, insert appropriate punctuation marks and symbols, and watch their own translation closely to correct any problems on the spot.

"I try to stay informed about what's going on in the world," Sheri Smargon says, "not just in the news. It helps to know that Eminem has a new record, as well as to know that Kosovo is a province, not a city."

EXPLORING

Although some core classes on captioning technology are being injected into court reporting and other stenographic curricula around the country, it is still a "hit or miss" situation, with many schools simply intimidated by the new technology. Good programs exist, however, that are providing beneficial exposure and actually working with local TV stations and area colleges to provide both news captioning and real-timing or steno interpreting in the classroom for deaf students and those with disabilities.

A smart way to prepare for real-time captioning, according to a real-time captioner who hires new graduates for a captioning company, is to practice by transcribing or writing newspaper articles or those from news magazines. Along with helping to build vocabulary skills, this exercise enables you to focus on conflict resolution by seeing the word in print, helps to familiarize you with difficult foreign names and words, and increases awareness of current events, both national and international.

While honing your skills, you may also get good exposure by working with local organizations such as the Association of Late-Deafened Adults, the Hearing Loss Association of America, the National Association of the Deaf, the Alexander Graham Bell Association for the Deaf and Hard of Hearing, and other nonprofit groups that might eventually need captioning services. Although the pay will not be as high as it would be at a captioning house, the job-satisfaction level will be significant. It is important to keep in mind that while the major captioning companies do sometimes hire people with little or no training for internships or on-the-job training, there is no substitute for experience.

EMPLOYERS

Captioners are employed primarily by captioning companies such as the NCI and VITAC. These companies contract with broadcasters and production companies to caption live and recorded events. Captioners work either as full-time employees for captioning companies or as freelancers (that is, independent contractors).

STARTING OUT

You should seek employment at one of the few large captioning companies in the country or contact station managers at your local television stations to inquire about real-time captioning positions. As with many other businesses, the best approach may be simply to start calling the leading companies in the field and the local companies and see who is hiring.

Before securing a real-time captioning position, you may have to "audition" as part of a pre-interview screening process that involves preparing raw steno notes from a sample tape-recorded program. The notes are then analyzed, with employment consideration based on the results of the evaluation and job experience. A good way to prepare for employment evaluation is to practice on the kind of material you wish to caption and to offer to demonstrate your skills.

ADVANCEMENT

Advancement for a real-time captioner is dependent upon performance, with salary increases and promotions to more responsible positions awarded with greater proficiency and tenure. Skilled real-time captioners may advance to supervisory positions.

EARNINGS

Earning power for real-time captioners is dependent upon many variables and is often region-specific and a product of "what the market will bear." In large captioning organizations, real-time captioners can make anywhere from $30,000 for a recent graduate in training to $65,000 or even higher for experienced and tireless workers who always volunteer for extra hours, overflow work, and so on and are capable of captioning all kinds of programming. Trainee salaries increase once the captioner goes on the air.

Salaries for real-time captioners are often in line with salaries for court reporters. The median annual income for all court reporters was $42,720 in 2004, according to the U.S. Department of Labor. Ten percent of reporters were paid less than $23,730 annually, and 10 percent had annual earnings of more than $78,840, also in 2004. A fringe benefit of working for a captioning agency for most reporters (particularly students just out of school) is that such agencies generally provide all the equipment, which costs approximately $15,000. Large captioning organizations also offer benefits, such as vacation and health insurance, likely to be provided at a courthouse for court reporters but not at a freelance firm of deposition reporters, for instance.

WORK ENVIRONMENT

Real-time captioning for television broadcast is not a nine-to-five job. While many reporting jobs require erratic hours, broadcast captioning is done seven days a week, around the clock. Real-time captioners producing captions for television broadcast will likely work nights, weekends, or holidays, as directed. Shows can air at 5:30 in the morning, at midnight on a Saturday, or during Thanksgiving dinner.

Given the irregularity of TV schedules, several shifts are needed to cover programming hours scheduled throughout the day. It is imperative that captioners be flexible and dependable and that they not get fatigued, so they can maintain high accuracy levels. How many hours a day a captioner is on the air depends on the level of experience. If new to the air, captioners may do only one or two shows a day, as it takes longer to prepare for a broadcast and review the result in the beginning. An experienced captioner may be on the air three to five hours a day, writing short programs or a news broadcast or sporting event. In the broadcast setting, real-time captioners do not have to produce transcripts, which eliminates the long hours that go along with that aspect of reporting.

Real-time captioning work can be physically demanding. Along with suffering the mental stress of performing in a live environment, real-time captioners may also be subject to repetitive stress injury, a prevalent industrial hazard for those who perform repeated motions in their daily work. Carpal tunnel syndrome, a type of repetitive stress injury, sometimes afflicts real-time captioners after several years. It can cause prickling sensation or numbness in the hand and sometimes a partial loss of function.

"Captioning and real-timing are totally different from regular court reporting," Sheri Smargon says. "You have to be a certain kind of person to real-time. I find captioning challenging and rewarding and fun, usually."

OUTLOOK

Although voice and speech systems that automatically convert speech to written text have been developed, no current systems can accurately handle multiple speakers, and it's unlikely that such technology will exist in the near future. Therefore, captioners and court reporters will be in high demand for years to come. Requirements by the Federal Communications Commission have also increased demand for captioners. The Telecommunications Act of 1996, for example, requires that all new programming on television be captioned.

Digital TV (DTV) will also make captioning more desirable and useful to more people, thereby increasing demand for captioners. DTV enhancements will allow viewers with poor vision to adjust text-size, styles, and fonts. DTV will also allow for more non-English letters, as well as more information transmitted per minute.

Captioners should focus first on the area where they want to live and work. To caption area news or city council meetings in a local area or do conventions in a large hotel, captioners must first obtain some costly supplies. These include a laptop or notebook computer, a compatible steno writer, cables, Internet hardware and software, and captioning software. Captioners may also need a character generator to project onto a large convention screen.

Captioners should learn the basic real-time skills that will enable them to do any live translating or interpreting on the computer. With such skills, they will be eligible for a variety of positions, including working in a computer-integrated courtroom; taking real-time depositions for attorneys; providing accompanying litigation support such as keyword indexing; real-timing or captioning in the classroom; or doing broadcast captioning. The future looks great for those who qualify themselves to perform real-time translation.

Other opportunities for the real-time captioner include working with hospitals that specialize in cochlear implants. For late-deafened adults who learned English before sign language, if they've learned to sign at all, captions provide a far greater comprehension level. Additionally, some local news stations across the country are working to expand and improve the quality of their local captioning capabilities, providing yet another source of potential employment for the real-time captioner.

FOR MORE INFORMATION

For information on digital/electronic court reporting and certification, contact
American Association of Electronic Reporters and Transcribers
23812 Rock Circle
Bothell, WA 98021-8573
Tel: 800-233-5306
Email: aaert@blarg.net
http://www.aaert.org

The NCI's Web site features historical information, a list of captioning terms, and employment information.
National Captioning Institute (NCI)
1900 Gallows Road, Suite 3000
Vienna, VA 22182-3874
Tel: 703-917-7600
http://www.ncicap.org

Visit the NCRA's Web site for extensive career and certification information, as well as information about technology, education programs, and access to the NCRA monthly magazine.
National Court Reporters Association (NCRA)
8224 Old Courthouse Road
Vienna, VA 22182-3808
Tel: 800-272-6272
Email: msic@ncrahq.org
http://www.ncraonline.org

For tips on preparing for certification exams and for other career information, contact
National Verbatim Reporters Association
207 Third Avenue
Hattiesburg, MS 39401-3868
Tel: 601-582-4345
Email: nvra@aol.com
http://www.nvra.org

Gary Robson, a leading professional in the world of captioning, maintains an extremely informative Web site, which features a Closed Captioning FAQ page and an informative overview of captioning.
Gary Robson's Closed Captioning FAQ
http://www.robson.org/capfaq

Reporters

OVERVIEW

Reporters are the foot soldiers for television and radio broadcast companies and print and online publications. They gather and analyze information about current events and write stories for publication or broadcasting. News analysts, reporters, and correspondents hold about 64,000 jobs in the United States.

HISTORY

Instantaneous worldwide communication became a reality in 1895 when an Italian engineer, Guglielmo Marconi, demonstrated how to send communication signals without the use of wires. Small radio shows started in 1910; in 1920, two commercial radio stations went on the air, and by 1921, a dozen local stations were broadcasting. The first network radio broadcast (more than one station sharing a broadcast) was of the 1922 World Series. By 1926, stations across the country were linked together to form the National Broadcasting Company (NBC). Four years later, the first radio broadcast was made around the world.

Modern television developed from experiments with electricity and vacuum tubes in the mid-1800s, but it was not until 1939, when President Franklin D. Roosevelt used television to open the New York World's Fair, that the public realized the power of television as a means of communication. Several stations went on the air shortly after this demonstration and successfully televised professional baseball games, college football games, and the Republican and Democratic conventions of 1940. The onset

QUICK FACTS

School Subjects
English
Journalism

Personal Skills
Communication/ideas
Helping/teaching

Work Environment
Indoors and outdoors
Primarily multiple locations

Minimum Education Level
Bachelor's degree

Salary Range
$18,340 to $46,290 to
$68,880+

Certification or Licensing
None available

Outlook
More slowly than the
average

DOT
131

GOE
11.08.02

NOC
5123

O*NET-SOC
27-3022.00

of World War II limited the further development of television until after the war.

Since television's strength is the immediacy with which it can present information, news programs became the foundation of regular programming. "Meet the Press" premiered in 1947, followed by nightly newscasts in 1948. People who bought early TV sets just for the novelty of it or to gather everyone around the tiny, snowy screen to see a favorite niece sing on a locally broadcast talent show were soon rewarded by the rapid expansion of the industry in the 1950s. The Federal Communications Commission lifted a freeze on the processing of station applications, and the number of commercial stations grew steadily, from 120 in 1953 to the 2,218 television stations of 2006.

It was in the 1960s and ensuing decades that television's power became most apparent: Together the country mourned the death of President Kennedy, witnessed the murder of his alleged assassin, Lee Harvey Oswald, by Jack Ruby, and formed opinions on the Vietnam War based on live TV news footage. The successes and failures of NASA programs brought viewers together, from the first steps on the moon, to the famous, near-fatal mission of Apollo 13; to the first space shuttle launch, to the tragic explosions of the *Challenger* and *Columbia*. In recent years, Americans were riveted and horrified as they watched the terrorist attacks (and their aftermath) unfold in New York City and Washington, D.C., on September 11, 2001.

But the big three networks (NBC, ABC, and CBS), which, along with PBS, reigned for many years as primary sources of information and entertainment for millions of people in the United States, have consistently lost viewers to cable, satellite TV, the Internet, and movie rentals. This hasn't stopped new networks, such as FOX and the CW Television Network (a conglomeration of the popular independent networks UPN and WB), from developing and competing. And although more and more people are looking to the World Wide Web as a source of information, people still rely on television and radio as trustworthy sources of news and quality entertainment. In addition, television and radio stations are using the Internet as another tool to provide information and entertainment to the public. Today, most television and radio stations have a strong presence on the Internet.

THE JOB

Reporters collect information on newsworthy events and prepare stories for radio or television broadcasts. The stories may simply provide information about local, state, or national events or may present opposing points of view on issues of current interest. In the latter capacity, the press plays an important role in monitoring the actions of public officials and others in positions of power. (Note: Reporters are also employed by newspapers and magazines, but this article focuses solely on opportunities for reporters in broadcasting.)

Stories may originate as an assignment from an editor or as the result of a lead (or news tip). Good reporters are always on the lookout for good story ideas. To cover a story, they gather and verify facts by interviewing people involved in or related to the event, examining documents and public records, observing events as they happen, and researching relevant background information. Reporters generally take notes or use a tape recorder as they collect information and write their stories once they return to their offices. In order to meet a deadline, they may have to telephone the stories to *rewriters,* who write or transcribe the stories for them. After the facts have been gathered and verified, the reporters transcribe their notes, organize their material, and determine what emphasis, or angle, to give the news. The story is then written to meet prescribed standards of editorial style and format.

The basic functions of reporters are to observe events objectively and impartially, record them accurately, and explain what the news means in a larger, societal context. Within this framework, there are several types of reporters.

Reporters may have specific areas, or "beats," to cover, such as a police station or city hall. Or they may be assigned specific regions within the viewing area. Though most reporters, particularly in radio, are required to cover all the news stories, some stations and newscasts have reporters who focus on particular subject matter—a reporter may specialize in reports on crime, technology, health care, entertainment, or business. Most reporters only report on that day's news, but, in some cases, a reporter may spend several days with a particular news story, such as on a news magazine program. An investigative report might also be broadcast as a series within a daily newscast.

The four major networks (ABC, CBS, NBC, and FOX) offer daily news coverage of events of national interest; there are also cable channels (such as CNN and MSNBC) that provide around-the-clock news information. With bureaus in Washington, D.C., New York, and other cities, the networks provide job opportunities for many reporters. These positions are highly competitive, however; most broadcast reporters work in cities all across the country for network affiliates, local cable news channels, or radio news stations.

Tim Russert, host of NBC's *Meet the Press*, interviews President Bush in the Oval Office. *(Landov)*

Some reporters gather and report news in foreign countries. This type of reporter is called a *foreign correspondent.* Foreign news can range from the violent (wars, coups, and refugee situations) to the calm (cultural events and financial issues). Although a domestic correspondent is responsible for covering specific areas of the news, such as politics, health, sports, consumer affairs, business, or religion, foreign correspondents are responsible for all of these areas in the country where they are stationed. A China-based correspondent, for example, could spend a day covering the new trade policy between the United States and China and the next day reporting the religious persecution of Christians by the Chinese government.

A foreign correspondent often is responsible for more than one country. Depending on where he or she is stationed, the foreign correspondent might have to act as a one-person band in gathering and preparing stories.

REQUIREMENTS

High School
High school courses that will provide you with a firm foundation for a reporting career include English, journalism, history, social stud-

ies, political science, geography, communications, typing, and computer science. Speech courses will help you hone your interviewing skills, which are necessary for success as a reporter. In addition, it will be helpful to take college prep courses such as foreign language, math, and science. Working for your high school newspaper or radio station will provide you with valuable experience interviewing, editing, and writing. Also, become familiar with video and recording equipment by working for your high school's media department. Contact a local reporter and ask to spend a few days shadowing him or her to get a sense of the work involved.

Postsecondary Training

You will need at least a bachelor's degree to become a reporter, and a graduate degree will give you a great advantage over those entering the field with lesser degrees. Most employers prefer applicants with degrees in broadcast journalism because their studies include liberal arts courses as well as professional training in journalism. Some employers consider it sufficient for a reporter to have a good general education from a liberal arts college. Others prefer applicants with an undergraduate degree in liberal arts and a master's degree in journalism. The great majority of journalism graduates hired today have majored specifically in broadcast journalism.

Approximately 200 colleges offer programs in broadcast journalism programs leading to a bachelor's degree. Broadcast programs require students to take courses such as reporting, photography, ethics, and broadcast history. Many schools also have TV and radio stations that either employ students or offer students credit for their work.

Journalism courses and programs are also offered by many community and junior colleges. Graduates of these programs are prepared to go to work directly as general assignment reporters, but they may encounter difficulty when competing with graduates of four-year programs. Credit earned in community and junior colleges may be transferable to four-year programs in journalism at other colleges and universities. Journalism training may also be obtained in the armed forces. The Accrediting Council on Education in Journalism and Mass Communications can provide you with information on journalism schools at its Web site: http://www.ku.edu/~acejmc/student/proglist.shtml.

A master's degree in journalism may be earned at approximately 120 schools and a doctorate at about 35 schools. Graduate degrees may prepare students specifically for careers in news or as journalism teachers, researchers, and theorists or for jobs in advertising or public relations.

A reporter's liberal arts training should include courses in English (with an emphasis on writing), sociology, political science, economics, history, psychology, business, speech, and computer science. Knowledge of foreign languages is also useful. Being a reporter in a specialized field such as science or finance requires concentrated course work in that area.

Other Requirements

Reporters are level-headed and able to keep calm in stressful situations. In most situations, reporters going live are required to think on their feet. Reporters must also have a good understanding of topical issues, history, geography, and government. And reporters must write and speak well.

You must also be inquisitive, assertive, persistent, and detail oriented. Also, you should enjoy interaction with people of various races, cultures, religions, economic levels, and social statuses.

EXPLORING

You can explore a career as a reporter in a number of ways. You can talk to reporters and editors at local radio and TV stations. You can also interview the admissions counselor at the school of journalism closest to your home.

In addition to taking courses in English, journalism, social studies, speech, computer science, and typing, high school students can acquire practical experience by working on school newspapers or on a church, synagogue, or mosque newsletter. Part-time and summer jobs on newspapers provide invaluable experience to the aspiring reporter.

College students can develop their reporting skills in the laboratory courses or workshops that are part of the journalism curriculum. College students might also accept jobs as campus correspondents for selected newspapers or college radio or television stations. People who work as part-time reporters covering news in a particular area of a community are known as *stringers* and are paid only for printed stories.

More than 3,000 journalism scholarships, fellowships, and assistantships are offered by universities, newspapers, foundations, and professional organizations to college students. Many broadcasting companies offer summer internships to journalism students to provide them with practical experience in a variety of basic reporting

Learn More About It

Boyd, Andrew. *Broadcast Journalism: Techniques of Radio and TV News*. Burlington, Mass.: Focal Press, 2000.

Edwards, Bob. *Edward R. Murrow and the Birth of Broadcast Journalism*. Hoboken, N.J.: John Wiley & Sons, 2004.

Ellis, Elmo. *Opportunities in Broadcasting Careers*. New York: McGraw-Hill, 2004.

Freedman, Wayne. *It Takes More Than Good Looks To Succeed at TV News Reporting*. Los Angeles: Bonus Books, 2003.

Hewitt, Don. *Tell Me a Story: Fifty Years and 60 Minutes in Television*. New York: PublicAffairs, 2003.

Keller, Teresa, and Stephen A. Hawkins. *Television News: A Handbook for Writing, Reporting, Shooting, and Editing*. Scottsdale, Ariz.: Holcomb Hathaway, Publishers, 2001.

Shook, Frederick. *Television Field Production and Reporting*. 4th ed. Boston: Allyn & Bacon, 2004.

and editing duties. Students who successfully complete internships are usually placed in jobs more quickly upon graduation than those without such experience.

EMPLOYERS

Of the approximately 64,000 reporters and correspondents employed in the United States, approximately 25 percent work in radio and television broadcasting. A small number are self-employed, working on a project or freelance basis or on their own publications and broadcasts.

STARTING OUT

Jobs in this field may be obtained through college career services offices or by applying directly to the personnel departments of individual employers. If you have some practical experience, you will have an advantage; you should be prepared to present a portfolio of material you wrote as a volunteer or part-time reporter or be able to present other writing or broadcast samples.

Most journalism school graduates start out as general assignment reporters in small media markets. A few outstanding journalism graduates may be hired by broadcasting companies in large media markets. They are trained on the job. But they are the exception, as large employers usually require several years' experience.

ADVANCEMENT

For those willing to relocate, advancement means moving up into a larger market or into network news. Within a local TV or radio station, a reporter may eventually move on to another area of broadcasting, such as directing or producing a newscast. Reporters also become anchors, who are better paid and more prominent in the newscast. Many more people are employed in sales, promotions, and planning than are employed in reporting and anchoring; and people in sales and management positions often draw a better salary than the journalists.

Many reporters transfer the contacts and knowledge developed in broadcast reporting to related fields such as public relations or advertising or by preparing copy for radio and television news programs. Others pursue opportunities in print media.

EARNINGS

There are great variations in the earnings of reporters. Salaries are related to experience, the type of employer for which the reporter works, geographic location, and whether the reporter is covered by a contract negotiated by a union.

According to the U.S. Department of Labor, the median salary for reporters and correspondents employed in all fields ranged from less than $18,340 to more than $68,880 in 2004. The U.S. Department of Labor reported that reporters and correspondents who worked in radio and television broadcasting had mean annual earnings of $46,290 in 2004.

WORK ENVIRONMENT

Reporters work under a great deal of pressure in settings that differ from the typical business office. Television and radio newsrooms can be hectic places. Reporters have to work amid the clatter of computer keyboards and other machines, loud voices engaged in telephone conversations, and the bustle created by people hurrying about. An atmosphere of excitement prevails, especially as broadcast deadlines approach. Since most stations broadcast 24 hours a day, reporters sometimes work around the clock to cover breaking stories.

Travel is often required in this occupation, and some assignments may be dangerous, such as covering wars, political uprisings, fires, floods, and other events of a volatile nature.

OUTLOOK

Employment for reporters and correspondents is expected to grow more slowly than the average for all occupations through 2014, according to the *Occupational Outlook Handbook*. Despite this prediction, newsrooms provide TV stations with healthy profits every year, and this is not expected to change. TV reporters will continue to be in demand; the number of news departments and news staff is expected to increase at a steady rate. But the number of students graduating from broadcast journalism departments is also growing. There are currently about 200 broadcast journalism programs in the country, and their students don't account for all the reporters seeking work in broadcasting; because news directors hire graduates from many different programs (and some prefer to hire graduates with a liberal arts degree), there's growing competition for the available positions.

Salaries are likely to stay low for broadcast reporters. With the large number of applicants for reporting positions, news directors can have their choice of the best without having to pay much. News directors are still not entirely happy with the graduates of broadcast journalism programs—studies done by such organizations as The Society of Professional Journalists and The Freedom Forum report that news directors believe today's reporters can't write well and don't have sufficient understanding of current affairs, history, and geography. Studies such as these may result in radical changes in journalism education and also in news department hiring practices.

Technology has a big impact on the way news is reported. The development of satellite technology and portable video cameras has revolutionized broadcast journalism over the last 25 years, and new developments over the next 20 years will likely have the same powerful effects. As the Internet competes for TV's viewers and radio's listeners, look for newsrooms to make better use of the technology. Many radio stations are broadcasting over the Web, and many TV stations have Web pages that feature up-to-the-minute local news coverage.

FOR MORE INFORMATION

Contact AWRT for information on careers in radio and television, as well as scholarships and internships.

American Women in Radio and Television (AWRT)
8405 Greensboro Drive, Suite 800
McLean, VA 22102-5120
Tel: 703-506-3290
Email: info@awrt.org
http://www.awrt.org

This organization provides general educational information on all areas of journalism, including newspapers, magazines, television, and radio.

Association for Education in Journalism and Mass
　Communication
234 Outlet Pointe Boulevard
Columbia, SC 29210-5667
Tel: 803-798-0271
Email: aejmchq@aejmc.org
http://www.aejmc.org

Visit the BEA's Web site for useful information about broadcast education and the broadcasting industry.

Broadcast Education Association (BEA)
1771 N Street, NW
Washington, DC 20036-2891
Tel: 888-380-7222
Email: beainfo@beaweb.org
http://www.beaweb.org

For information on union membership, contact

National Association of Broadcast Employees and Technicians
Email: nabet@nabetcwa.org
http://nabetcwa.org

For broadcast education, support, and scholarship information, contact

National Association of Broadcasters
1771 N Street, NW
Washington, DC 20036-2891
Tel: 202-429-5300
Email: nab@nab.org
http://www.nab.org

Contact the society for information on student chapters, scholarships, educational information, discussion groups, and much more.

Society of Professional Journalists
Eugene S. Pulliam National Journalism Center
3909 North Meridian Street
Indianapolis, IN 46208-4011
Tel: 317-927-8000
http://spj.org

——————— INTERVIEW ———————

Sarah McCurdy has been a reporter at KVLY/KXJB (an NBC/CBS duopoly) in Fargo, North Dakota, for nearly three years. She was kind enough to discuss her career with the editors of Careers in Focus: Broadcasting.

Q. Why did you decide to enter this career?

A. I've always had an interest in communications and the media. I'm a "people person," and from the time I was young it seemed like a natural fit. Just before my 16th birthday I got a job at a local radio station working weekends and fill-in shifts. I worked at KNDK radio in Langdon, North Dakota, through high school and came back for two summers in college.

Q. How did you train for this career? What was your educational path?

A. I started out doing radio in high school. After graduation I attended Concordia College in Moorhead, Minnesota. I graduated with a B.A. in mass communications. The television profession is one where you need to complete an internship. After my semester-long internship, I got a full-time job.

Q. Please describe a typical day on the job.

A. Typically I get to work between 7:30 and 8 A.M. when I work the day shift. I read the paper, check my email, flip through my file of story ideas, and call/visit people on my beat. I cover education so I check in with people at school district offices and local universities. We have our morning meeting in the newsroom at 8:40. That's when the news director, assignment editor, executive producers, reporters, and photographers get together to pitch story ideas and talk about what's going on around the community that day. After each reporter has an assignment, we start making calls and lining up interviews. We are paired with a photographer and we go out and gather video and interviews. When we get back to the newsroom I log and write my stories. We are usually LIVE either in the field or in the studio. Then you come in the next day and start over.

Q. What are the pros and cons of being a reporter?

A. Pros: I love the "people" part of my job. I love being able to meet new people every day. You will find in this career that with the good and the bad stories, anyone who talks to you on camera trusts you enough to let you tell their story. With this job you always have a "pass" to be front and center when the action is happening.

Cons: At your first job as a reporter don't expect to make much money. It will be enough to live on, but you'll have to be good at making a budget and sticking to it. If you don't like stress and deadlines, this might be a tough world for you to enter. We have six newscasts from the afternoon through the evening, as well as a morning show, that we have to find enough stories to fill. We are all responsible for helping that happen. Sometimes things change right when you're getting somewhere with your story, and you have to drop it and move on to something else. And sometimes you have to interview people who you may not want to interview.

Q. Where do you see yourself professionally in five or 10 years?

A. That's a question I've been asking myself lately, too! I really enjoy Fargo, and I have worked really hard to become a respected reporter. I have a lot of contacts and sources here, and I enjoy teaching younger people, so in five years I see myself continuing at KVLY. I enjoy the people and the job. We have a good team. On the other hand, I may try to move up markets—that's always another option. There are some incredible "storytelling" stations and markets out there; that's where I would want to be.

Sports Broadcasters and Announcers

OVERVIEW

Sports broadcasters, or *sportscasters*, for radio and television stations select, write, and deliver footage of current sports news for the sports segment of radio and television news broadcasts or for specific sports events, channels, or shows. They may provide pregame and postgame coverage of sports events, including interviews with coaches and athletes, as well as play-by-play coverage during the game or event.

Sports announcers are the official voices of the teams. At home games, the sports announcer makes pregame announcements, introduces the players in the starting lineups, and keeps the spectators in the stadium or arena abreast of the details of the game by announcing such things as fouls, substitutions, and goals and who is making them.

HISTORY

Radio signals, first transmitted by Guglielmo Marconi in 1895, led to early experimentation with broadcasting in the years preceding World War I. After the war began, however, a ban on amateur, nonmilitary radio broadcasts delayed radio's acceptance. In 1919, when the ban was lifted, hundreds of amateur stations sprang up. By 1922, 500 were licensed by the government. Codes and domestic broadcast wavelengths were assigned by the government, which created a traffic jam of aerial signals. Eventually, more powerful stations were permitted to broadcast at a higher wavelength, provided these

QUICK FACTS

School Subjects
English
Journalism
Speech

Personal Skills
Communication/ideas
Leadership/management

Work Environment
Indoors and outdoors
Primarily multiple locations

Minimum Education Level
Some postsecondary training

Salary Range
$14,000 to $35,000 to
$2,000,000+

Certification or Licensing
None available

Outlook
More slowly than the
average

DOT
159

GOE
01.03.03

NOC
5231

O*NET-SOC
27-3011.00

stations only broadcast live music. This move by the government quickly brought entertainment from large, urban areas to the small towns and rural areas that characterized most of the United States at the time.

In the early days of radio broadcasts, anyone who operated the station would read, usually verbatim, news stories from the day's paper. Quickly, station managers realized that the station's "voice" needed as much charisma and flair as possible. Announcers and journalists with good speaking voices were hired. With the arrival of television, many of those who worked in radio broadcasting moved to this new medium.

Corporate-sponsored radio stations weren't long in coming; Westinghouse Corporation and American Telephone and Telegraph (AT&T) raced to enter the market. Westinghouse engineer Frank Conrad received a license for what is viewed as the first modern radio station, KDKA, in Pittsburgh, Pennsylvania. KDKA broadcast music programs, the 1920 presidential election, and sports events. The next year, Westinghouse began to sell radio sets for as little as $25. By 1924, the radio-listening public numbered 20 million.

Meanwhile, as early as 1929, Vladimir Kosma Zworykin, a Soviet immigrant employed by Westinghouse, was experimenting with visual images to create an all-electronic television system. By 1939 the system was demonstrated at the New York's World Fair with none other than President Franklin D. Roosevelt speaking before the camera. World War II and battles over government regulation and AM and FM frequencies interrupted the introduction of television to the American public, but by 1944, the government had determined specific frequencies for both FM radio and television.

In 1946, the number of television sets in use was 6,000; by 1951, the number had risen to an astonishing 12 million. Unknowingly, the stage had been set for a battle between radio and television. In the ensuing years, expert after expert predicted the demise of radio. The popularity of television, its soap operas, family dramas, and game shows, was believed by nearly everyone to be too strong a competitor for the old-fashioned, sound-only aspect of radio. The experts proved wrong; radio flourished well into the 1990s, when the industry experienced some cutbacks in the number of stations and broadcast hours because of recession.

The national radio networks of the early days are gone, but satellites allow local stations to broadcast network shows anywhere with the equipment to receive the satellite link. The development of filmed and videotaped television, cable and satellite transmissions, broadcasting deregulation, and an international market through direct broadcast satellite systems has drastically changed the face and future of both radio and television.

Today's sports broadcasters in radio and television have all these technological tools and more at their fingertips. Want to see an instant replay of the game-winning three-point shot by Kobe Bryant? As the sportscaster describes it, a technician is playing it back for the viewing public. Have to travel to Costa Rica for a business trip, but hate to miss that Yankees game? No problem. A sportscaster is giving the play-by-play to an AM network station that is, in turn, sending it via satellite to a Costa Rican client-station.

THE JOB

One of the primary jobs of most sportscasters for both radio and television stations is to determine what sports news to carry during a news segment. The sportscaster begins working on the first broadcast by reading the sports-related clippings that come in over the various news wire services, such as Associated Press and United Press International. To follow up on one of these stories, the sportscaster might telephone several contacts, such as a coach, scout, or athlete, to see if he or she can get a comment or more information. The sportscaster also might want to prepare a list of upcoming games, matches, and other sports events. Athletes often make public appearances for charity events and the sportscaster might want to include a mention of the charity and the participating athlete or athletes.

After deciding which stories to cover and the lineup of the stories that will be featured in the first of the day's broadcasts, sportscasters then review any audio or video clips that will accompany the various stories. Sportscasters working for radio stations choose audio clips, usually interviews, that augment the piece of news they will read. Sportscasters working for television stations look for video footage—the best 10 seconds of this game or that play—to demonstrate why a certain team lost or won. Sometimes sportscasters choose footage that is humorous or poignant to illustrate the point of the news item.

After they decide which audio or video segments to use, sportscasters then work with sound or video editors to edit the data into a reel or video, or they edit the footage into a tape themselves. In either case, the finished product will be handed over to the news director or producer with a script detailing when it should play. The news producer or director will make certain that the reel or video comes in on cue during the broadcast.

Frequently a sportscaster will make brief appearances at local sports events to interview coaches and players before and after the game, and sometimes during breaks in the action. These interviews, as well as any footage of the game that the station's camera crews obtain, are then added to the stock from which sportscasters choose for their segments.

Usually, the main broadcast for both radio and television sportscasters is the late-evening broadcast following the evening's scheduled programming. This is when most of the major league sports events have concluded, the statistics for the game are released, and final official scores are reported. Any changes that have occurred since the day's first sports broadcast are updated and new footage or sound bites are added. The final newscast for a television sportscaster will most likely include highlights from the day's sports events, especially dramatic shots of the most impressive or winning points scored.

In televised sports news, the emphasis is on image. Often, sportscasters, like other newscasters, are only on camera for several seconds at a time, but their voices continue over the videotape that highlights unique moments in different games.

For many sportscasters who work in television, preparing the daily sportscasts is their main job and takes up most of their time. For others, especially sportscasters who work in radio, delivering a play-by-play broadcast of particular sports events is the main focus of their job. These men and women use their knowledge of the game or sport to create with words a visual picture of the game, as it is happening, for radio listeners. The most common sports for which sportscasters deliver play-by-play broadcasts are baseball, basketball, football, and hockey. A few sportscasters broadcast horse races from the racetrack and sometimes these broadcasts are carried by off-track betting facilities.

Sportscasters who give the play-by-play for a basketball game, for example, usually arrive an hour or so before the start of the game. Often they have a pregame show that features interviews with, and a statistical review of, the competing teams and athletes. To broadcast a basketball game, sportscasters sit courtside in a special media section so that they can see the action up close. During football, baseball, and hockey games sportscasters usually sit in one of the nearby media boxes. Throughout the game sportscasters narrate each play for radio listeners using rapid, precise, and lively descriptions. During time-outs, halftimes, or other breaks in play, sportscasters might deliver their own running commentaries of the game, the players' performances, and the coaching.

The sportscaster who specializes in play-by-play broadcasts needs to have an excellent mastery of the rules, players, and statistics of a sport, as well as the hand signals officials use to regulate the flow of a game. Some sportscasters provide play-by-play broadcasts for several different teams or sports, from college to professional levels, requiring them to know more than one sport or team well.

Some sportscasters, often former athletes or established sports personalities, combine the two aspects of the job. They act as anchors or coanchors for sports shows and give some play-by-play commentary while also providing their television or radio audience with statistics and general updates.

Sports announcers provide spectators with public address announcements before and during a sports event. For this job, announcers must remain utterly neutral, simply delivering the facts—goals scored, numbers of fouls, or a time-out taken. Sports announcers may be sportscasters or they may be professional announcers or emcees who make their living recording voice-overs for radio and television commercials and for large corporations or department stores.

Sports announcers usually give the lineups for games, provide player names and numbers during specific times in a contest, make public announcements during time-outs and pauses in play, and generally keep the crowd involved in the event (especially in baseball). Baseball announcers may try to rally the crowd or start the crowd singing or doing the wave.

REQUIREMENTS

High School
Graduating from high school is an important first step on the road to becoming a sports broadcaster or announcer. While in school, take classes that will allow you to work on your speaking and writing skills. Classes in speech, English, journalism, and foreign languages, such as Spanish and French, will be helpful. You may also find it helpful to take courses in drama and computer science.

Postsecondary Training
Educational requirements for sportscasting positions vary depending on the position. Competition for radio and television sports broadcasting positions is especially fierce, so any added edge can make the difference.

Television sportscasters who deliver the news in sports usually have bachelor's degrees in communications or journalism, although personality, charisma, and overall on-camera appearance is so important to ratings that station executives often pay closer attention to the taped auditions they receive from prospective sportscasters than to the items on resumes. Prepare for the job by learning a sport inside and out, developing valuable contacts in the field through internships and part-time or volunteer jobs, and earning a degree in journalism or communications. It also should be noted that the industry is finicky and subjective about looks and charisma.

It is not as crucial for sportscasters who deliver play-by-play broadcasts for radio stations to have the journalistic skills that a television sportscaster has, although good interviewing skills are essential. Instead, they need excellent verbal skills, a daunting command of the sport or sports that they will be covering, and a familiarity with the competing players, coaches, and team histories. To draw a complete picture for their listeners, sportscasters often reach back into history for an interesting detail or statistic, so a good memory for statistics and trivia and knowledge of sports history are helpful.

Other Requirements
A nice speaking voice, excellent verbal and interviewing skills, a pleasant appearance, a solid command of sports in general as well as in-depth knowledge of the most popular sports (football, basketball, baseball, and hockey), and an outgoing personality are all necessary for a successful career in sportscasting.

In addition, you need to have a strong voice, excellent grammar and English usage, and the ability to ad-lib when doing so is necessary.

EXPLORING

High school and college students have many opportunities to investigate this career choice, but the most obvious way is to participate in a sport. By learning a sport inside and out, you can gain valuable insight into the movements and techniques that you will be describing as a sportscaster. In addition, firsthand experience and a love of the sport itself makes it easier to remember interesting trivia related to the sport and the names and numbers of the pros who play it.

If you do not have the coordination or skill for the sport itself, you can volunteer to help out with the team by shagging balls, running drills, or keeping statistics. The latter is perhaps the best way to learn the percentages and personal athletic histories of athletes.

An excellent way to develop the necessary communications skills is to take a journalism course, join the school's speech or debate team, deliver the morning announcements, work as a DJ on the school radio station, or volunteer at a local radio station or cable television station.

Arizona Diamondbacks television broadcasters Mark Grace (left) and Thom Brennaman conduct their pre–game program before a baseball game. *(Landov)*

John Earnhardt from the National Association of Broadcasters has this advice: "Write about your school's sports teams for your school newspaper or hometown newspaper and read, read, read about sports. Knowledge about the area you are interested in reporting about is the best tool for success. It is also necessary to be able to express yourself well through the spoken word. Speaking before an audience can be the best practice for speaking before the camera or on a microphone."

Finally, you can hone your sportscasting skills on your own while watching your favorite sports event by turning down the sound on your television and tape-recording your own play-by-play deliveries.

EMPLOYERS

Most sports broadcasters work for television networks or radio stations. The large sports networks also employ many broadcasters. John Earnhardt says, "The main employers of sports broadcasters are sports networks that own the rights to broadcast sporting events and the broadcast stations themselves." Radio sportscasters are hired by radio stations that range from small stations to mega-stations.

Sports announcers work for professional sports arenas, sports teams, minor league and major league ball teams, colleges, universities, and high schools.

Because sports are popular all over the country, there are opportunities everywhere, although the smaller the town, the fewer the opportunities. "Larger cities generally have more opportunities because of the number of stations and the number of sports teams that need to be covered," Earnhardt says.

STARTING OUT

Although an exceptional audition tape might land you an on-camera or on-air job, most sportscasters get their start by writing copy, answering phones, operating cameras or equipment, or assisting the sportscaster with other jobs. Internships or part-time jobs will give you the opportunity to become comfortable in front of a camera or behind a microphone. Of course, contacts within the industry come in handy. In many cases, it is simply an individual's devotion to the sport and the job that makes the difference—that and being in the right place at the right time. John Earnhardt adds that knowledge is key as well. "It obviously helps to know the sport you are reporting on—first, one needs to study the sport and know the sport's rules, history, and participants better than anyone," he advises.

Put together an audio tape (if you are applying for a radio job or an announcer position) or a videotape (for television jobs) that showcases your abilities. On the tape, give your account of the sports events that took place on a certain day.

ADVANCEMENT

In the early stages of their careers, sportscasters might advance from a sports copywriter to actual broadcaster. Later in their careers, sportscasters advance by moving to larger and larger markets, beginning with local television stations and advancing to one of the major networks.

Sportscasters who work in radio may begin in a similar way; advancement for these individuals might come in the form of a better time slot for a sports show or the chance to give more commentary.

Sports announcers advance by adding to the number of teams for whom they provide public address announcements. Some sports announcers also may start out working for colleges and minor leagues and then move up to major league work.

EARNINGS

Salaries in sportscasting vary, depending on the medium (radio or television), the market (large or small, commercial or public), and whether the sportscaster is a former athlete or recognized sports celebrity, as opposed to a newcomer trying to carve out a niche. According to a salary survey conducted by the Radio-Television News Directors Association (RTNDA) and Ball State University, television sports anchors, salaries range from a low of $16,000 to a high of $1,000,000, with a median salary of $35,000. For radio sports anchors, salaries range from a low of $14,000 to a high of $50,000, with a median salary of $29,500.

Salaries are usually higher for former athletes and recognized sports personalities or celebrities, such as ex-coaches like John Madden. These individuals already have an established personality within the sports community and may thus have an easier time getting athletes and coaches to talk to them. Salaries for such recognizable personalities can be $2,000,000 or more per year.

WORK ENVIRONMENT

Sportscasters usually work in clean, well-lighted booths or sets in radio or television studios or in special soundproof media rooms at the sports facility that hosts sports events.

Time constraints and deadlines can create havoc and add stress to an already stressful job; often, a sportscaster has to race back to the studio to make the final evening broadcast. Sportscasters who deliver play-by-play commentary for radio listeners have the very stressful job of describing everything going on in a game as it happens. They cannot take their eyes off the ball and the players while the clock is running and this can be nerve-wracking and stressful.

On the other hand, sportscasters are usually on a first-name basis with some of the most famous people in the world, namely, professional athletes. They quickly lose the star-struck quality that usually afflicts most spectators and must learn to ask well-developed, concise, and sometimes difficult questions of coaches and athletes.

Sports announcers usually sit in press boxes near the action so they can have a clear view of players and their numbers when announcing. Depending on the type of sport, this may be an enclosed area or out in the open air. Sports announcers start announcing before the event begins and close the event with more announcements but then are able to end their workday. Because sporting events are scheduled at many different times of the day, announcers sometimes must be available at odd hours.

OUTLOOK

Competition for jobs in sportscasting will continue to be fierce, with better-paying jobs in larger markets going to experienced sportscasters who have proven they can keep ratings high. Sportscasters who can easily substitute for other on-camera newscasters or anchors may be more employable.

The projected employment outlook is one of slower-than-average growth, as not that many new radio and television stations are expected to enter the market. Most of the job openings will come as sportscasters leave the market to retire, relocate, or enter other professions. In general, employment in this field is not affected by economic recessions or declines; in the event of cutbacks, on-camera sports broadcasters and announcers are the last to go.

FOR MORE INFORMATION

To read more about the sportscasting field, including current news, interviews with working professionals, and profiles of all-time sportscasting greats, visit
American Sportscasters Association
225 Broadway, Suite 2030
New York, NY 10007-3742
Tel: 212-227-8080
Email: info@americansportscastersonline.com
http://www.americansportscastersonline.com

For a list of schools that offer programs and courses in broadcasting, contact
Broadcast Education Association
1771 N Street, NW
Washington, DC 20036-2891
Tel: 888-380-7222
Email: beainfo@beaweb.org
http://www.beaweb.org

The FCC offers information on media guidelines, including all radio laws. For more information, contact
Federal Communications Commission (FCC)
445 12th Street, SW
Washington, DC 20554-0001
Tel: 888-225-5322
Email: fccinfo@fcc.gov
http://www.fcc.gov

To get general information about broadcasting, contact
National Association of Broadcasters
1771 N Street, NW
Washington, DC 20036-2891
Tel: 202-429-5300
Email: nab@nab.org
http://www.nab.org

For career information and helpful Internet links, contact
Radio-Television News Directors Association
1600 K Street, NW, Suite 700
Washington, DC 20006-2838
Tel: 202-659-6510
Email: rtnda@rtnda.org
http://www.rtnda.org

——— INTERVIEW ———

Pete Byrne is a sports anchor/reporter for KVLY-TV, the NBC affiliate in Fargo, North Dakota. He talked with the editors of Careers in Focus: Broadcasting *about his career and breaking into the field of sports broadcasting.*

Q. Tell us about yourself.
A. I've been broadcasting sport professionally for six years, the past three in Fargo. I anchor the nightly 6:00 P.M. and 10:00 P.M. sportscasts during the weekends and report on sporting events during the week. This includes shooting games for highlight purposes, and interviewing coaches and athletes to put together packages for our daily casts. In addition, I'm the sideline reporter for North Dakota NBC Sports, which broadcasts all of the North Dakota state tournament games in football, basketball, and ice hockey. I also provide sideline reports for

occasional NCAA football broadcasts of games in the region, and do television play-by-play for the Fargo-Moorhead Red-Hawks minor league baseball team.

Q. What advice would you give to students looking to enter the field?

A. My advice to students, high school or college, with an interest in sportscasting is to START NOW! If you wait until a month before you graduate from college, you're years behind the rest of your peers. If sports are your interest and you play them in high school, keep playing. If you don't play, find a way to get involved with any media-type activity. If there's a student radio station or student paper, sign up. In some areas, I've seen cable-access channels broadcast high school games with students doing the play by play. I knew a guy who used to take a tape recorder to games and called the game onto an audiocassette just for practice. It works. ANYTHING you can do that simulates the real thing is beneficial.

I also suggest that you call up your local TV or radio sports anchor, tell them you're interested in getting into the field, and ask to meet with him or her. Be flexible. We're usually fairly busy, so meet when they are available. Ask your questions, LISTEN to what they say, and if you still like it, inquire about an internship. If you do get an internship, it's important to tell your boss what you're interested in, but you also need to take direction and help out even if they have you doing things that don't particularly interest you. The station is going to provide you with valuable work experience. As you learn, you will provide free/cheap labor. We teach all of our interns how to operate a camera and shoot highlights. More often than not, that's what they do for us. We understand that you want to be an anchor, not a photographer, but you probably won't be getting on the air as an intern. What the sports anchor does looks easy, and he/she makes it look easy because they've had years of practice. Here's what you can do: Try a few practice anchor demos during your internship. You'll learn what it's like to be on the desk in front of the camera, and you'll have a resume/demo tape to send out when you are done. This is how it works. You make a demo, put it on a tape, and send it out to stations looking to hire young sportscasters. Here's the key: All the highlight shooting and editing you did while you were an intern, even though you didn't like it, will set you apart. Chris Berman has the luxury of having a team of producers, writers, and editors put his show together for him. You won't. Demonstrating the ability to put your own show together, including shooting your own highlights, will tell news directors that you are capable of doing the job he or she needs you to do.

The bottom line is that the more you can learn, and the sooner you can learn it, the more attractive candidate you are. Be energetic, take direction, and be persistent. Lots of kids want that job, and only one will get it. Don't get discouraged. It doesn't matter if 100 stations don't want you to be their sports anchor. All that matters is the one station that does!

Talent Agents
and Scouts

OVERVIEW

An agent is a salesperson who sells artistic or athletic talent. *Talent agents* act as representatives for actors, directors, writers, models, athletes, and other people who work in the arts, advertising, sports, and fashion. (This article focuses primarily on agents in broadcasting, including film.) Agents promote their clients' talent and manage their legal contractual business. Approximately 10,000 agents and business managers of artists, performers, and athletes are employed in the United States.

HISTORY

The wide variety of careers that exist in the television and film industries today evolved gradually. In the 19th century in England and America, leading actors and actresses developed a system, called the "actor-manager system," in which the actor both performed and handled business and financial arrangements. Over the course of the 20th century, responsibilities diversified. In the first decades of the century, major studios took charge of the actors' professional and financial management.

In the 1950s the major studio monopolies were broken, and control of actors and contracts came up for grabs. Resourceful business-minded people became agents when they realized that there was money to be made by controlling access to the talent behind movie and television productions. They became middlemen between actors

QUICK FACTS

School Subjects
Business
Mathematics

Personal Skills
Communication/ideas
Leadership/management

Work Environment
Primarily indoors
Primarily one location

Minimum Education Level
Bachelor's degree

Salary Range
$25,420 to $55,140 to
$86,000+

Certification or Licensing
None available

Outlook
Faster than the average

DOT
191

GOE
11.12.03

NOC
5124

O*NET-SOC
13-1011.00

(and other creative people) and the production studios, charging commissions for use of their clients.

Currently, commissions range between 10 and 15 percent of the money an actor earns in a production. In more recent years, agents have formed revolutionary deals for their stars, making more money for agencies and actors alike. Powerful agencies such as Creative Artists Agency, International Creative Management, and the William Morris Agency are credited with (or, by some, accused of) heralding in the age of the multimillion-dollar deal for film stars.

In addition to representing film and television actors, producers, directors, and other creative professionals, agents also represent well-known radio personalities such as Howard Stern, sports stars, popular musicians, and top executives in the broadcasting and motion picture industries.

THE JOB

Talent agents act as representatives for actors, writers, radio personalities, and others who work in the entertainment industry. They look for clients who have potential for success and then work aggressively to promote their clients to film and television directors, casting directors, production companies, broadcasting companies, advertising companies, and other potential employers. Agents work closely with clients to find assignments that will best achieve clients' career goals.

Agents find clients in several ways. Those who work for an agency might be assigned a client by the agency, based on experience or a compatible personality. Some agents also work as *talent scouts* and actively search for new clients, whom they then bring to an agency. Or the clients themselves might approach agents who have good reputations and request their representation. Agents involved in the broadcasting industries review portfolios, screen tests, and audiotapes to evaluate potential clients' appearance, voice, personality, experience, ability to take direction, and other factors.

When an agent agrees to represent a client, they both sign a contract that specifies the extent of representation, the time period, payment, and other legal considerations.

When agents look for jobs for their clients, they do not necessarily try to find as many assignments as possible. Agents try to carefully choose assignments that will further their clients' careers. For example, an agent might represent an actor who wants to work in television, but is having difficulty finding a role. The agent looks for roles in commercials, music videos, or voice-overs that will give the actor some exposure.

Agents also work closely with the potential employers of their clients. They need to satisfy the requirements of both parties. For example, agents who represent actors have a network of directors, producers, advertising executives, and photographers that they contact frequently to see if any of their clients can meet their needs.

When agents see a possible match between employer and client, they speak to both and quickly organize meetings, interviews, or auditions so that employers can meet potential hires and evaluate their work and capabilities. Agents must be persistent and assertive on behalf of their clients. They spend time on the phone with employers, convincing them of their clients' talents and persuading them to hire clients. There may be one or several interviews, and the agent may coach clients through this process to make sure clients understand what the employer is looking for and adapt their presentations accordingly. When a client achieves success and is in great demand, the agent receives calls, scripts, and other types of work requests and passes along only those that are appropriate to the interests and goals of the client.

When an employer agrees to hire a client, the agent helps negotiate a contract that outlines salary, benefits, promotional appearances, and other fees, rights, and obligations. Agents have to look out for the best interests of their clients and at the same time satisfy employers in order to establish long-lasting relationships.

In addition to promoting individuals, agents may also work to make package deals—for example, combining a writer, director, and a star to make up a package, which they then market to production studios. The agent charges a packaging commission to the studio in addition to the commissions agreed to in each package member's contract. A strong package can be very lucrative for the agency or agencies who represent the talent involved, since the package commission is often a percentage of the total budget of the production.

Agents often develop lifelong working relationships with their clients. They act as business associates, advisers, advocates, mentors, teachers, guardians, and confidantes. Because of the complicated nature of these relationships, they can be volatile, so a successful relationship requires trust and respect on both sides, which can only be earned through experience and time. Agents who represent high-profile talent make up only a small percentage of agency work. Most agents represent lesser-known or locally known talent.

The largest agencies are located in Los Angeles and New York City, where broadcasting, film, theater, advertising, publishing, fashion, and art-buying industries are centered. There are modeling and theatrical agencies in most large cities, however, and independent agents are established throughout the country.

REQUIREMENTS

High School

You should take courses in business, mathematics, and accounting to prepare for the management aspects of an agent's job. Take English and speech courses to develop good communication skills because an agent must be gifted at negotiation. You also need a good eye for talent, so you need to develop some expertise in radio, television, film, theater, art, literature, advertising, sports, or whatever field you hope to specialize in.

Postsecondary Training

There are no formal requirements for becoming an agent, but a bachelor's degree is strongly recommended. Advanced degrees in law and business are becoming increasingly prevalent; law and business training are useful because agents are responsible for writing contracts according to legal regulations. However, in some cases an agent may obtain this training on the job. Agents come from a variety of backgrounds; some of them have worked as actors and then shifted into agent careers because they enjoyed working in the industry. Agents who have degrees from law or business schools have an advantage when it comes to advancing their careers or opening a new agency.

Other Requirements

It is most important to be willing to work hard and aggressively pursue opportunities for clients. You should be detail-oriented and have a good head for business; contract work requires meticulous attention to detail. You need a great deal of self-motivation and ambition to develop good contacts in industries that may be difficult to break into. You should be comfortable talking with all kinds of people and be able to develop relationships easily. It helps to be a good conversationalist in addition to being knowledgeable about your field.

EXPLORING

To learn more about working as an agent in the film and television industries, read publications agents read, such as *Radio & Records* (http://www.radioandrecords.com), *Daily Variety* (http://www.variety.com), *The Hollywood Reporter* (http://www.hollywoodreporter.com), *Premiere* (http://www.premiere.com), and *Entertainment Weekly* (http://www.ew.com). Listen to radio personalities to learn more about top talent in this industry. Watch current television shows and movies to get a sense of the established and up-and-coming talents in these industries. Trace the careers of actors you like, including their early work in independent films, commercials, and stage work.

If you live in Los Angeles or New York City, you may be able to volunteer or intern at an agency to find out more about the career. If you live outside Los Angeles and New York City, check your phone book's Yellow Pages, or search the Web, for listings of local agencies. Most major cities have agents who represent local performing artists, radio personalities, actors, and models. If you contact them, they may be willing to offer you some insight into the nature of talent management in general.

EMPLOYERS

Approximately 10,000 agents and business managers of artists, performers, and athletes are employed in the United States. Talent agencies are located all across the United States, handling a variety of talents. Those agencies that represent artists and professionals in the television and film industries are located primarily in Los Angeles. Some film agencies, such as The William Morris Agency, are located in New York City. An agency may specialize in a particular type of talent, such as minority actors, extras, or TV commercial actors. The top three film agencies—Creative Artists Agency, International Creative Management, and the William Morris Agency—employ approximately 1,500 agents. The radio industry is centered in New York City, so many agencies that represent radio personalities are located there.

STARTING OUT

The best way to enter this field is to seek an internship with an agency. If you live in or can spend a summer in Los Angeles or New York City, you have an advantage in terms of numbers of opportunities. Libraries and bookstores will have resources for locating talent agencies. By searching the Web, you can find many free listings of reputable agents. The Screen Actors Guild also maintains a list of franchised agents that is available on its Web site. The Yellow Pages will yield a list of local talent agencies. For those who live in Los Angeles, there are employment agencies that deal specifically with

talent agent careers. Compile a list of agencies that may offer internship opportunities. Some internships will be paid and others may
provide college course credit; most important, they will provide you
with experience and contacts in the industry. An intern who works
hard and knows something about the business stands a good chance
of securing an entry-level position at an agency. At the top agencies,
this will be a position in the mail room, where almost everyone
starts. In smaller agencies, it may be an assistant position. Eventually persistence, hard work, and cultivated connections will lead to
a job as an agent.

ADVANCEMENT

Once you have a job as an assistant, you will be allowed to work
closely with an agent to learn the ropes. You may be able to read contracts and listen in on phone calls and meetings. You will begin to
take on some of your own clients as you gain experience. Agents who
wish to advance must work aggressively on behalf of their clients as
well as seek out quality talent to bring into an agency. Those who
are successful command more lucrative salaries and may choose to
open their own agencies. Some agents find that their work is a good
stepping stone toward a different career in the industry.

EARNINGS

Earnings for agents vary greatly, depending on the success of the
agent and his or her clients. An agency receives 10 to 15 percent of a
client's fee for a project. An agent is then paid a commission by the
agency as well as a base salary. The U.S. Department of Labor reports
the following mean annual salaries for agents and business managers in 2004 by specialty: cable and other subscription programming,
$91,490; agents and managers for public figures, $77,190; and independent artists, writers, and performers, $81,230. Salaries for agents
and business managers of artists, performers, and athletes ranged
from less than $25,420 to more than $86,000 annually.

Working for an agency, an experienced agent will receive health and
retirement benefits, bonuses, and paid travel and accommodations.

WORK ENVIRONMENT

Work in a talent agency can be lively and exciting. It is rewarding to
watch a client attain success with your help. The work can seem very
glamorous, allowing you to rub elbows with the rich and famous and

make contacts with the most powerful people in the entertainment industry. Most agents, however, represent less-famous actors, radio personalities, directors, and other industry professionals.

Agents' work requires a great deal of stamina and determination in the face of setbacks. The work can be extremely stressful, even in small agencies. It often demands long hours, including evenings and weekends. To stay successful, agents at the top of the industry must constantly network. They spend a great deal of time on the telephone, with both clients and others in the industry, and attending industry functions.

OUTLOOK

Employment in the arts and entertainment field is expected to grow rapidly in response to the demand for entertainment from a growing population. However, the numbers of artists and performers also continues to grow, creating fierce competition for all jobs in this industry. This competition will drive the need for more agents and scouts to find talented individuals and place them in the best jobs.

Despite a plethora of entertainment options available today, the American public retains a strong love of television shows and movies. With markets overseas expanding and the increasing popularity of DVD sales, even the television shows and films that don't do so well domestically can still turn a tidy profit. As a result, agents at all levels in these industries will continue to thrive. Also, more original cable television programming will lead to more actors and performers seeking representation.

FOR MORE INFORMATION

Visit the SAG Web site for information about acting in films, television shows, and music videos and for a list of talent agencies.
Screen Actors Guild (SAG)
5757 Wilshire Boulevard
Los Angeles, CA 90036-3600
Tel: 323-954-1600
http://www.sag.com

Television Directors

OVERVIEW

Television directors have ultimate control over the decisions that shape a TV production. The director is an artist who coordinates the elements of a television show and is responsible for its overall style and quality. Television directors work on a variety of productions. For example, they may work on local news programs, cover national sporting events, or tape commercials for businesses. And with the development of "narrowcasting" (broadcasting meant for limited viewing, such as for classrooms, hospitals, or corporations), some directors create programming for very small audiences. Directors are well known for their part in guiding actors and other TV professionals, but they are involved in much more, such as casting, costuming, cinematography, editing, and sound recording. Every television project, no matter how short or how small the intended audience, requires a director.

HISTORY

Drama developed in societies all over the world and dates back thousands of years. Playwrights and actors strove to impress, educate, and influence audiences with their dramatic interpretations of stories. From these ancient beginnings until the early half of the 19th century, actors directed themselves in productions. Until that time, it had been common practice for one of the actors involved in a production to be responsible not only for his or her own performance but also for conducting rehearsals and coordinating the tasks involved in putting on a play. Usually the most experienced and respected troupe member would guide the other actors, providing advice on speech, movement, and interaction.

A British actress and opera singer named Madame Vestris is considered to have been the first professional director. In the 1830s Vestris leased a theater in London and staged productions in which she herself did not perform. She displayed a new, creative approach to directing, making bold decisions about changing the traditional dress code for actors and allowing them to express their own interpretations of their roles. Vestris coordinated rehearsals, advised on lighting and sound effects, and chose nontraditional set decorations; she introduced props such as actual windows and doors that were more realistic than the usual painted panoramas.

By the turn of the century, theater directors such as David Belasco and Konstantin Stanislavsky had influenced the way in which performances were given, provoking actors and actresses to strive to identify with the characters they revealed so that audiences would be passionately and genuinely affected. By the early 1900s, Stanislavsky's method of directing performers had made an overwhelming mark on drama. His method (now often referred to as "the Method"), as well as his famous criticism, "I do not believe you," continue to influence performers to this day.

By the early 20th century, the film industry had also begun its rapid growth, and directors joined the teams of professionals who contributed to the production of movies. Commercial television, first available in the mid-1940s, provided yet another medium for directors, actors, and other professionals to work with. As a variety of television shows developed—dramas, newscasts, talk shows, for example—and the number of television stations multiplied, new opportunities opened up for television directors. Today, some TV directors work on a freelance basis, completing different projects for various production companies; others work for special interest cable channels, such as ESPN or MTV; still others work for network affiliates across the country. No matter what the project, however, all directors have one thing in common: They direct the talents and skills of a number of professionals, bringing together all the pieces to create a complete program.

THE JOB

The television director's responsibilities are varied and often depend on the project. For example, the director of a TV movie, documentary, or an episode of a series will have more control over the final production than the director of a news broadcast or a live event.

The TV director working on a movie will use a script, go through rehearsals with actors, and shoot and reshoot scenes from many perspectives. To achieve the intended mood of the piece—such as dark and gloomy for a mystery—the director carefully orchestrates the work of lighting and sound technicians, camera operators, and editors. With such a production, the director can take the time to polish the final product that the audience will see.

A director covering a live event, such as a football game, has much less control over the outcome. In this case, the director only gets one shot at broadcasting the game. The director's responsibilities may include working with announcers to make sure their equipment is functioning properly; stationing camera operators so that they are positioned correctly to cover any possible play the teams might make; and being ready to introduce graphics, such as charts with player statistics. The director has little room for error when covering a live event.

Richard Perry, a director/editor for WWAY TV-3 in Wilmington, North Carolina, directs the 5:30 P.M. newscast. News directors may need to combine working from a script and arranged order of stories with the unpredictability of covering a live event. In addition, the news director's job isn't limited to the actual broadcast; he or she must also direct promotional segments, news updates, and some videotaped segments to accompany the live reports later. Although Perry directs the evening news, he reports to work at 5:00 A.M. to help prepare for the daily morning show as well as to direct the various updates and promotions to be broadcast throughout the day.

One of the first things Perry does every morning is make the graphics for the morning news and, as he says, "I prep the 'supers'." Supers are superimposed words that run across the TV screen and provide information such as the names of interview subjects. The newsroom sends a printed list of these supers to Perry. He then types the names and titles into the chryon (the character generator), making sure everything is spelled correctly and in the right order. From 6:00 to 7:00 A.M., Perry runs the chryon for the morning show. This involves hitting the control for running the words across the screen at the right time. From 7:00 to 8:30 A.M., Perry directs the local weather and news cut-ins for broadcasting during *Good Morning, America.*

After his morning work, Perry is usually able to take a break. He returns to the station midafternoon and often spends a couple of hours working on commercial production; then he begins preproduction for the evening news. "We make graphics for over-the-shoulder shots," he explains, "and put boards on tape for the news editors to put in their stories." Boards are graphics and lists of information. These boards are videotaped and then edited by the reporter directly into news packages (or self-contained stories on tape, consisting of the reporter's audio and edited video). In the half hour before the evening news, Perry goes over the script, which has information about the order stories will be shown and who is covering them.

During the broadcast, the director typically sits in the control room and wears a headset through which he or she can communicate with the producer and TV crew. The director gives orders to keep the broadcast running smoothly and on time. Large TV stations have both a director and a technical director—a member of the technical crew who works directly with the cameras and other equipment and may make adjustments on the control board. But in a smaller station like Perry's, directors take on many responsibilities. "I sit in front of the switcher," Perry says, "and tell everyone what to do and push all the right buttons at the right time so the show looks smooth." He tells the camera people what to shoot next and calls for tapes to be played (or "rolled") during the broadcast.

Freelance directors may work on live or taped productions. In addition to their responsibilities as directors—coordinating the work of crews, deciding on shots, overseeing editing—they may also need to take on many other elements involved in production. For example, they may need to work on getting funding for a project, hiring writers and assistants, or setting up locations for filming. They may even be involved in publicizing the project and entering it in festivals or competitions. In addition to all these responsibilities, freelance directors must also continually promote themselves and look for new projects to work on. The workflow for a freelance director can be unpredictable. They often take on a variety of projects, covering anything from sporting events to beauty pageants, in order to maintain a steady work schedule.

REQUIREMENTS

High School

The sooner you can get to know a camera and how to set up interesting shots, the better. If your high school offers courses about media or television production, be sure to take those. You should also consider taking photography classes that will teach you about the composition of an image. Take English and journalism classes that will hone your communication skills and give you a feeling for completing assignments on deadline. Computer classes that teach you how to work with graphics programs will be beneficial. If you are considering working as a freelancer, take mathematics, business, or accounting classes to help you manage your business. If you're interested in live directing and working with actors and story scripts, take drama classes to gain experience in this area.

Postsecondary Training

Although a college degree isn't necessarily required of a TV director, it does give you an edge in the workplace. Also, many colleges have internship programs and career services that can help you get your foot in the door of the professional world. If you're interested in working for a TV news station, you should apply to the broadcast departments of journalism schools.

If you're interested in directing dramas or sitcoms for network and cable TV, you may want to enroll in a drama school to develop a theater background and experience working with scripts and actors. A number of universities and colleges also offer film studies programs or courses on television broadcast production. Your guidance counselor should be able to help you locate these. Also, do research on your own by checking out school Web sites and reading books about directing.

No matter what college program you enroll in, however, one of your top goals should be to gain hands-on experience through an

College broadcast journalism students produce a public affairs program in a campus news studio. (*Jim Whitmer Photography*)

internship at a TV station. You will probably not be paid for your work, but you may be able to get course credit. Some schools offer internship opportunities.

Organizations may also be a source of information on internships. The Radio-Television News Directors Association, for example, offers a limited number of scholarships and internships. The Directors Guild of America sponsors several training programs. One of these, the New York Assistant Director Training Program, lasts two years and the participants gain experience shooting on locations in New York City and Los Angeles. Competition for these programs is extremely fierce. A summer fellowship at the International Radio and Television Foundation offers an all-expense paid program, which includes career-planning advice and practical experience at a New York-based corporation. They also offer a minority career workshop, which brings college students to New York for orientation in electronic media.

Other Requirements

Those who want to be television directors should be strong leaders. "You have to be in order to pull together so many people to this one common goal: getting the show on the air cleanly," says Richard Perry. Directors also must be able to concentrate in a hectic environment. Perry notes, "I have an ability to focus on whatever is before me and to block out everything else that is unnecessary."

A director also needs self-confidence as well as the ability to work with other people. Personality conflicts sometimes arise between producers and directors or other members of the production team. The director needs to be able to mediate differences and bring people together.

Though you can work for a small station without union membership, the networks and major markets require you to be represented by the Directors Guild of America (DGA). The DGA represents film and TV directors, assistant directors, and others. With membership, you'll have access to health care benefits and legal representation. The DGA also offers awards to members and promotes the hiring of minorities and women.

EXPLORING

Join your high school newspaper staff to become familiar with reporting and editing. Volunteer to act as a staff photographer. If your high school has its own TV station, join the production crew. You might be able to videotape school events or work on the school

Learn More About Careers in Television

Abramson, Albert. *The History of Television, 1880 to 1941*. Jefferson, N.C.: McFarland & Company, 1987.
Abramson, Albert. *The History of Television, 1942 to 2000*. Jefferson, N.C.: McFarland & Company, 2003.
Crouch, Tanja L. *100 Careers in Film and Television*. Hauppauge, N.Y.: Barrons Educational Series, 2002.
Ellis, Elmo. *Opportunities in Broadcasting Careers*. New York: McGraw-Hill, 2004.
Richards, Andrea. *Girl Director: A How-To Guide for the First-Time, Flat-Broke Film and Video Maker*. Berkeley, Calif.: Ten Speed Press, 2005.

newscast. Also, consider getting involved with the drama club. You may not want to be the star of the school play, but you can be involved in production work and may be able to videotape the play for the drama archives.

Contact a local TV station and ask for a tour of the facilities. Explain that you are interested in working as a director and ask to meet with one during your tour. Or set up a separate appointment for an informational interview with a director. Go to the interview prepared to ask questions about the work and the director's experience. People are often happy to talk about their work if you show a genuine interest.

EMPLOYERS

Television directors may work as salaried full-time employees for network or network-affiliated stations, cable stations, businesses, or agencies, or they may work as freelancers. Freelancers are not full-time employees of a particular company. Instead, freelancers work on a project-by-project basis for different employers (for example, doing one project for a network and another for an advertising agency).

STARTING OUT

The position of director is not an entry-level job. You will need to work your way up through the ranks, gaining experience and knowledge along the way. Internships provide the best way to enter this competitive field. The internship gives you hands-on experience and the opportunity to make contacts within the industry. Richard Perry's internship as a production assistant during college led to his permanent position with WWAY-TV. "I gradually worked my way up through prompter, camera, tapes, audio, and finally I was a director." Perry also worked part time for the station for three-and-a-half years before being hired full time.

Other starting-out possibilities include working as an assistant for a freelance director or video production company. Be prepared to take any position that will give you hands-on experience with cameras and production, even if it's only on a part-time or temporary basis.

ADVANCEMENT

Advancement for television directors depends somewhat on their individual goals. One director might consider it an advancement to move from general TV programming to special interest programming. Another might feel that becoming a full-time freelancer is an advancement. Those who work at small stations tend to advance by relocating and working for larger stations. "If I want to move up as a director," Richard Perry says, "I'll have to move up to a larger market, maybe Charlotte or Raleigh." Such a move would mean receiving a larger salary and overseeing a bigger staff.

EARNINGS

Salaries vary greatly for TV directors and are determined by a number of factors. A director of a newscast at a small TV station will probably be at the low end of the scale, while a director working on a hit series for a network may earn hundreds of thousands of dollars a year. A freelance director working project-to-project may earn a great deal one year and much less the following year.

A 2002 salary survey by the Radio-Television News Directors Association found that television news directors had salaries that ranged from $18,000 to $250,000. The median annual salary was $64,000. Assistant news directors earned between $19,000 and $150,000. The median salary was $57,000. According to the U.S. Department of Labor, the mean yearly income for directors employed in radio and television was $55,400 in 2004.

Directors who work full time for stations or other organizations generally receive benefits such as health insurance and paid vacation and sick days.

WORK ENVIRONMENT

A TV station is a busy and exciting place where no two days are exactly alike. If the director is working on a live event, the atmosphere may be stressful and somewhat chaotic as he or she makes snap decisions, calls up the correct graphics, and keeps the show within the time limits. A director working on a taped project that will air at a later date may feel somewhat less "on air" stress; however, this director must also constantly pay attention to numerous production details, staying on budget and resolving problems among the staff. Because the director is responsible for clarifying what everyone's responsibilities for a project are, he or she may need to mediate in a tense situation. "Nine-to-five" definitely does not describe a day in the life of a director; twelve-hour days (and more) are not uncommon. Because directors are ultimately responsible for so much, schedules often dictate that they become immersed in their work around the clock, from preproduction to final cut. Nonetheless, those able to make it in the industry find their work to be extremely enjoyable and satisfying.

OUTLOOK

The U.S. Department of Labor predicts that employment growth for actors, producers, and directors will increase at an average rate through 2014. Those wanting to become directors should realize that many see the television industry as a glamorous field, and there will be stiff competition for jobs.

More TV programs are produced now than ever before, and this number should continue to grow. New technology will allow cable stations to offer hundreds of additional channels and therefore need more original programming. Also, as more businesses and organizations recognize that TV and video productions can educate the public about their work as well as train employees, they will need directors' services to complete new projects.

Newsrooms provide TV stations with healthy profits every year, and this is not expected to change. Therefore, directors will continue to be in demand to direct newscasts. Directors of traditionally less-recognized forms, such as commercials and music videos, are beginning to receive more name recognition.

In the future, the number of TV directors who work freelance will likely increase. As productions become more costly and as smaller networks produce original programming, hiring directors on a project-by-project basis is becoming more economical.

FOR MORE INFORMATION

To learn more about the industry and DGA-sponsored training programs and to read selected articles from DGA Magazine, contact
Directors Guild of America (DGA)
7920 Sunset Boulevard
Los Angeles, CA 90046-3304
Tel: 310-289-2000
http://www.dga.org

For more information on fellowships and other programs, contact
International Radio and Television Society
420 Lexington Avenue, Suite 1601
New York, NY 10170-1602
Tel: 212-867-6650
http://www.irts.org

This organization for electronic media news professionals has information on internships, scholarships, and the news industry.
Radio-Television News Directors Association
1600 K Street, NW, Suite 700
Washington, DC 20006-2838
Tel: 202-659-6510
Email: rtnda@rtnda.org
http://www.rtnda.org

This Web site contains links to numerous television-related sites and lists colleges and universities worldwide that offer training in television broadcast production.
CineMedia
http://www.cinemedia.org

Television Editors

OVERVIEW

Television editors perform an essential role in the television industry. They take an unedited draft of videotape and use specialized equipment to improve the draft until it is ready for viewing. It is the responsibility of the television editor to create the most effective product possible. Television editors may also be employed in the film industry. There are approximately 20,000 film, video, and television editors employed in the United States.

HISTORY

The television industry has experienced substantial growth in the last few decades. The effect of this growth is a steady demand for the essential skills that television editors provide. With recent innovations in computer technology, much of the work that editors perform is accomplished using sophisticated computer programs. All of these factors have enabled many television editors to find steady work as salaried employees of television production companies and as independent contractors who provide their services on a per-job basis.

In the early days of the industry, editing was sometimes done by directors, studio technicians, or others for whom this work was not their specialty. Now, every videotape, including the most brief television advertisement, has an editor responsible for the continuity and clarity of the project.

THE JOB

Television editors work closely with producers and directors throughout an entire project. These editors assist in the earliest phase, called preproduction, and during the production phase, when actual filming occurs. Their skills are in greatest demand during postproduction, the completion of primary filming. During preproduction, in meetings with producers, editors learn about the objectives of the film or video. If the project is a television commercial, for example, the editor must be familiar with the product the commercial will attempt to sell. If the project is a feature-length motion picture, the editor must understand the story line. The producer may explain the larger scope of the project so that the editor knows the best way to approach the work when it is time to edit the film. In consultation with the director, editors may discuss the best way to accurately present the screenplay or script. They may discuss different settings, scenes, or camera angles even before filming or taping begins. With this kind of preparation, film and television editors are ready to practice their craft as soon as the production phase is complete.

Feature-length films, of course, take much more time to edit than television commercials. Therefore, film editors may spend months on one project, while others may be working on several shorter projects simultaneously.

Steve Swersky owns his own editorial company in Santa Monica, California, and he has done editing for commercials, films, and TV. In addition to editing many Jeep commercials and coming-attractions trailers for such movies as *Titanic, Fargo,* and *The Usual Suspects,* Swersky has worked on 12 films. Though commercials can be edited quickly, a film project might take six to nine months to edit. Swersky's work involves taking the film that has been developed in labs and transferring it to videotape for him to watch. He uses "nonlinear" computer editing for his projects, as opposed to traditional "linear" systems involving many video players and screens. "The difference between linear and nonlinear editing," he says, "is like the difference between typing and using a word processor. When you want to change a written page, you have to retype it; with word processing you can just cut and paste." Swersky uses the Lightworks nonlinear editing system. With this system, he converts the film footage to a digital format. The computer has a database that tracks individual frames and puts all the scenes together in a folder of information. This information is stored on a hard drive and can instantly be brought up on a screen, allowing an editor to access scenes and frames with the click of a mouse.

Editors are usually the final decision-makers when it comes to choosing which segments will stay in as they are, which segments will be cut, or which may need to be redone. Editors look at the quality of the segment, its dramatic value, and its relationship to other segments. They then arrange the segments in an order that creates the most effective finished product. "I assemble the scenes," Swersky says, "choosing what is the best, what conveys the most emotion. I bring the film to life, in a way." He relies on the script and notes from the director, along with his natural sense of how a scene should progress, in putting together the film, commercial, or show. He looks for the best shots, camera angles, line deliveries, and continuity.

Some editors specialize in certain areas of television or film. *Sound editors* work on the soundtracks of television programs or motion pictures. They often keep libraries of sounds that they reuse for various projects. These include natural sounds such as thunder or raindrops, animal noises, motor sounds, or musical interludes. Some sound editors specialize in music and may have training in music theory or performance. Others work with sound effects. They may use unusual objects, machines, or computer-generated noisemakers to create a desired sound for a film or TV show.

REQUIREMENTS
High School
Broadcast journalism and other media and communications courses may provide you with practical experience in video editing. Because television editing requires a creative perspective along with technical skills, you should take English, speech, theater, and other courses that will allow you to develop writing skills. Art and photography classes will acquaint you with visual media. If you're lucky enough to attend a high school that offers film classes, either in film history or production, be sure to take those courses. Finally, don't forget to take computer classes. Editing work constantly makes use of new technology, and you should become familiar and comfortable with computers as soon as possible.

Postsecondary Training
Some studios require a bachelor's degree for those seeking positions as television editors. However, actual on-the-job experience is the best guarantee of securing lasting employment. Degrees in communications or liberal arts fields are preferred, but courses in cinematography and audiovisual techniques help editors get started in their work. You may choose to pursue a degree in such subjects as English, journalism, theater, art, or film. Community and two-year colleges often offer courses in the study of film as literature. Some of these colleges also teach video and film editing. Universities with

departments of broadcast journalism offer courses in video and film editing and also may have contacts at local television stations.

Training as a television editor takes from four to 10 years. Many editors learn much of their work on the job as an assistant or apprentice at larger studios that offer these positions. During an apprenticeship, the apprentice has the opportunity to see the work of the editor up close. The editor may eventually assign some of his or her minor duties to the apprentice, while the editor makes the larger decisions. After a few years, the apprentice may be promoted to editor or may apply for a position as a television editor at other studios. Training in video and film editing is also available in the military, including the Air Force, Marine Corps, Coast Guard, and Navy.

Other Requirements

You should be able to work cooperatively with other creative people when editing a project. You should remain open to suggestions and guidance, while also maintaining your confidence in the presence of other professionals. A successful editor has an understanding of the history of television and a feel for the narrative form in general. Computer skills are also important and will help you learn new technology in the field. You may be required to join a union to do this work, depending on the studio. "You should have a good visual understanding," Steve Swersky says. "You need to be able to tell a story, and be aware of everything that's going on in a frame."

EXPLORING

Many high schools have film clubs, and some have cable television stations affiliated with the school district. School-run television channels often give students the opportunity to actually create and edit short programs. Check out what's available at your school.

Believe it or not, a good way to prepare for a career as a television editor is to read. Reading literature will help develop your understanding of the different ways in which stories can be presented.

You should be familiar with all different kinds of television and film projects, including documentaries, short films, feature films, TV shows, and commercials. Observe as many different projects as you can and study them, paying close attention to the decisions the editors made in piecing together the scenes.

Large television stations occasionally have volunteers or student interns. Most people in the industry start out doing minor tasks helping with production. These production assistants get the opportunity to see all of the professionals at work. By working closely with an editor, a production assistant can learn television operations as well as specific editing techniques.

EMPLOYERS

Approximately 20,000 film, television, and video editors are employed in the United States. Some television editors work primarily with news programs, documentaries, or special features. They may develop ongoing working relationships with directors or producers who hire them from one project to another. Many editors who have worked for a studio or postproduction company for several years often become independent contractors. They offer their services on a per-job basis to producers of commercials and films, negotiating their own fees, and typically have purchased or leased their own editing equipment.

STARTING OUT

Because of the glamour associated with television work, this is a popular field that can be very difficult to break into. With a minimum of a high school diploma or a degree from a two-year college, you can apply for entry-level jobs in many television studios, but these jobs won't be editing positions. Most studios will not consider people for television editor positions without a bachelor's degree or several years of on-the-job experience.

One way to get on-the-job experience is to complete an apprenticeship in editing. However, in some cases you won't be eligible for an apprenticeship unless you are a current employee of the studio. Therefore, start out by applying to as many television studios as possible and take an entry-level position, even if it's not in the editing department. Once you start work, let people know that you are interested in an editor apprenticeship so that you'll be a potential candidate the next time one becomes available.

Those who have bachelor's or master's degrees have typically gained hands-on experience through school projects. Another benefit of going to school is that contacts that you make while in school, both through your school's placement office and alumni, can be a valuable resource when you look for your first job. Your school's placement office may also have listings of job openings. Some studio work is union regulated. Therefore, you may also want to contact union locals to find out about job requirements and openings.

ADVANCEMENT

Once television editors have secured employment in their field, their advancement comes with further experience and greater recognition. Some editors develop good working relationships with directors or producers. These editors may be willing to leave the security of a studio job for the possibility of working one-on-one with the director or producer on a project. These opportunities often provide editors with the autonomy they may not get in their regular jobs. Some are willing to take a pay cut to work on a project they feel is important.

Some editors choose to stay at their studios and advance through seniority to editing positions with higher salaries. They may be able to negotiate better benefits packages or to choose the projects they will work on. They may also choose which directors they wish to work with. In larger studios, they may train and supervise staffs of less-experienced or apprentice editors.

Some sound or sound-effects editors may wish to broaden their skills by working as general editors. Some television editors may, on the other hand, choose to specialize in sound effects, music, or some other editorial area. Some editors who work in television may move to motion pictures or may move from working on commercials or television series to working on television movies.

EARNINGS

Television editors are not as highly paid as others working in their industry. They have less clout than directors or producers, but they have more authority in the production of a project than many other film technicians. According to the U.S. Department of Labor, the mean annual wage for television editors was $45,180 in 2004. Salaries for film and television editors ranged from less than $22,250 to $98,790 or more in 2004. A 2002 salary survey by the Radio-Television News Directors Association found that television tape editors had salaries that ranged from $8,000 to $80,000, with a median salary of $23,000. The most experienced and sought-after television and film editors can command much higher salaries, even more than $150,000 a year.

WORK ENVIRONMENT

Most of the work editors perform is done in television studios or at postproduction companies using editing equipment. The working environment is often a small, cramped studio office. Working hours vary widely depending on the project. During the filming of a commercial, for instance, editors may be required to work overtime, at night, or on weekends to finish the project by an assigned date. "As stressful as the work can be," Steve Swersky says, "we joke around that it's not like having a real job. Every day is a fun day."

During filming, editors may be asked to be on hand at the filming location. Locations may be outdoors or in other cities, and travel is occasionally required. More often, however, the television or film editor edits in the studio, and that is where the bulk of the editor's time is spent.

Disadvantages of the job involve the editor's low rank on the totem pole of television-industry jobs. However, most editors feel that this is outweighed by the advantages. Television editors can view the projects on which they have worked and be proud of their role in creating them.

OUTLOOK

Employment for television and film editors will grow about as fast as the average for all occupations through 2014, according to the U.S. Department of Labor. The growth of cable television and an increase in the number of independent film studios will translate into greater demand for editors. This will also force the largest studios to offer more competitive salaries in order to attract the best television and film editors.

The developments of companies such as Avid Technology, which engineered and introduced many of the digital editing tools used today, will continue to greatly affect the editing process. Editors will work much more closely with special-effects houses in putting together projects. When using more effects, television and film editors will have to edit scenes with an eye toward special effects to be added later. Digital editing systems are also available for home computers. Users can feed their own digital video into their computers, then edit the material, and add their own special effects and titles. This technology may allow some prospective editors more direct routes into the industry, but the majority of editors will have to follow traditional routes, obtaining years of hands-on experience.

FOR MORE INFORMATION

The ACE features career and education information for film and television editors on its Web page, along with information about internship opportunities and sample articles from CinemaEditor Magazine.

American Cinema Editors (ACE)
100 Universal City Plaza
Verna Fields Building 2282, Room 190
Universal City, CA 91608-1002
Tel: 818-777-2900
http://www.ace-filmeditors.org

This union counts film and television production workers among its craft members. For education and training information as well as links to film commissions and production companies, check out the IATSE's Web site.
International Alliance of Theatrical Stage Employees, Moving
   Picture Technicians, Artists and Allied Crafts of the United
   States, Its Territories and Canada (IATSE)
1430 Broadway, 20th Floor
New York, NY 10018-3348
Tel: 212-730-1770
http://www.iatse-intl.org

For information on NATAS scholarships and to read articles from Television Quarterly, *the organization's official journal, visit the NATAS's Web site.*
National Academy of Television Arts and Sciences (NATAS)
111 West 57th Street, Suite 600
New York, NY 10019-2211
Tel: 212-586-8424
Email: hq@natasonline.com
http://www.emmyonline.org

Television Producers

OVERVIEW

Television producers are behind-the-scenes professionals involved with budgeting and financing, working out a production time line, casting appropriate actors, or even hiring the crew for a TV project. Producers oversee the production of newscasts, sporting events, dramas, comedies, documentaries, holiday specials, and the many other programs that make up network and cable broadcasting. Because of the varied nature of television programming, a producer's role may also change from project to project. A producer on one project, for example, may only be involved in arranging financial backing and putting together the creative team of directors and actors. A producer on another project may oversee practically every detail of the production, including arranging for equipment and scheduling personnel.

HISTORY

The position of television producer has its roots in two older forms of visual arts: drama and film. Drama has existed in cultures around the world for thousands of years. As drama and theaters developed, the roles of actors, writers, directors, and producers became clearly defined. The motion picture industry, which experienced rapid growth during the early 20th century, provided a new medium for artistic professionals to work in, and many positions, such as producer, were copied from the theater world.

In 1945, following World War II, commercial television broadcasting became available in the United States. The television industry experienced phenomenal growth through increasingly better equipment, more TV stations, and larger audiences. By 1949, for example,

QUICK FACTS

School Subjects
Business
English

Personal Skills
Communication/ideas
Leadership/management

Work Environment
Primarily indoors
Primarily one location

Minimum Education Level
Bachelor's degree

Salary Range
$26,940 to $55,400 to $200,000+

Certification or Licensing
None available

Outlook
About as fast as the average

DOT
159

GOE
01.03.01

NOC
5131

O*NET-SOC
27-2012.00

nearly 10 million people watched the inauguration of President Truman on television.

Naturally, professionals were needed to create, perform, and produce programming for this ever-growing new medium. This new opportunity drew producers from the film world and others who simply wanted to work with television. The producer became an essential member of production teams at small stations across the country as well as at large network stations. Today, with such factors as increasingly sophisticated equipment (for example, computers that can generate images), enormous salaries for popular TV stars (the cast of the show *Friends,* for example, each made $1 million per episode during the final season of the program), and a growing number of networks showing specialized programming (such as Oxygen and VH1), the job of the producer has become more complex. The producer must have a depth of technical knowledge, the ability to manage large financial sums, and an instinct for choosing projects that will draw large audiences.

THE JOB

Producers oversee television projects, from the idea stage to the final taped or aired version. Their responsibilities, however, vary depending on both the producer's employer and the project. One of the primary responsibilities of independent producers, those with their own production companies, may be to raise money for projects. A producer employed by a television station, on the other hand, may be given a budget to work with. In either case, though, the producer is responsible for keeping an eye on costs and making sure the project stays within budget. This also requires time-management skills, because the producer must schedule just the right amount of time for different phases of production. If the producer underestimates the time needed for filming on location, for example, the producer's company will need to pay the expenses for extra time on location, causing the project to go over budget.

A producer's responsibilities are also affected by what type of project he or she works on. For example, *newscast producers,* along with reporters, determine what stories are worth broadcasting. Newscast producers assign stories, review taped reports, and may even help edit the material. Often, these producers must deal with late-breaking developments and must quickly assign reporters and TV crews to cover a story and then weave the new report into the broadcast while staying within the broadcast's time requirements.

The newscast is a combination of live and taped segments, and the producer often needs to make decisions quickly while the show is on the air.

Documentary producers are also very actively involved in their productions, but they typically have days, rather than hours, to complete projects. They may be involved in deciding on a concept for the documentary; hiring writers, directors, and the crew; and scouting out locations and finding interview subjects. Once interviews and other segments are taped, they may review the material, select the best footage, and edit it into a program of predetermined length.

Whereas newscast and documentary producers rely on their news judgment, *drama* and *comedy producers* rely on their understanding of the entertainment world. These producers come up with ideas for shows; hire writers, directors, and actors; and review the final product for its tone and content.

Freddy James is an associate producer for Home and Garden Television (HGTV). He works on producing specials for this cable network, and his work often takes him away from the station for periods of time. One project he worked on focused on the Habitat for Humanity program, which recruits volunteers to build homes for families in need. James's work began long before the filming took place. "We pre-interviewed 10 families who were to receive homes and selected three [to focus on]," he says. "We centered the show on them and on the volunteers who came from all over the world to help them build these homes in one week."

With other members of the production, James planned the shoot. They set up all the hotel and crew arrangements, as well as researched the Habitat for Humanity program. They scheduled interviews with officials of Habitat for Humanity. "And we went to the families' old homes and interviewed them about the project and how they felt about being a part of it," James explains. During the four-day shoot, the production team got footage of the houses going up, and they talked to officials and volunteers. The on-air talent then arrived for a day to shoot his commentary.

Once all the filming was done, the producers returned to the station with all the footage and reviewed the material. "We select our bites," James says, "and start writing the show. Our executive producers proof our scripts, then we set up a voice-over session for our talent, and he voices the script." After selecting video for a program, the producers have it digitized for editing on the computer. On this project, the producers also worked with musicians who composed music for the show and graphic artists who created design work.

No matter what type of programming producers work on, they must be organized team leaders, able to communicate their ideas about a project from concept to conclusion.

REQUIREMENTS

High School

If working as a television producer interests you, there are a number of classes you can take in high school to help you get ready for this work. It will be very important for you to take composition, speech, and English classes to help you develop your research, writing, and speaking skills. These communication skills will be essential to have in your career. In addition, take mathematics, business, or accounting classes, since you will be managing budgets. Consider taking psychology classes that may give you an understanding of people and their interests. Take computer classes so that you can develop a familiarity with this tool. If your high school offers any classes on the history of broadcast media or the use of broadcast media, be sure to take those. If you are specifically interested in producing entertainment shows, consider taking drama classes that will give you an understanding of scripts and working with actors.

Postsecondary Training

While there are no formal educational requirements for becoming a television producer, many producers do have college degrees. The degree you get may depend on the area of television that you are interested in. For example, if you are interested in news broadcasting, you may want to consider attending a journalism school to receive a broadcast journalism degree. Make sure that you get a broad-based education, however. Anyone working in the news industry will need an understanding of history, geography, and political science, so take classes that cover these subjects as well.

If you are interested in producing a television series, you may want to attend a drama or film school. Programs at these schools will help you hone your understanding of story lines and audiences and markets. A number of universities and colleges also offer film studies programs or courses on television broadcast production. Ask your school guidance counselor to help you locate these programs.

In addition, do your own research. Check out the Web sites of schools you are interested in and read books on the topic. A number of producers have rounded out their education by taking business courses or even by completing a business degree along with their broadcast studies to prepare them for this career.

Perhaps the most important thing to consider when selecting a school is the internship opportunities that will be available to you. Some schools have their own broadcasting stations where you can work; others require students to complete an internship that they locate on their own; and still others may offer internships through local participating network affiliates. No matter what the arrangements, you should be sure the school you choose will provide you with a way to gain practical hands-on experience working at a TV station. Competition for internships is high, and most positions are unpaid. In some cases, though, you may be able to get course credit for your work.

A number of organizations provide information on internships or sponsor internship programs. The Radio-Television News Directors Association, for example, offers several scholarships and internships for college students involved with electronic journalism. The Institute on Political Journalism offers an eight-week summer program during which college students combine classroom work at Georgetown University with work at a Washington, D.C., media organization. The Directors Guild of America sponsors Los Angeles- and New York-based training programs for a limited number of college graduates. The trainees in this program are paid and work on television series projects. See the end of this article for contact information to learn more about these opportunities.

Other Requirements

The successful producer is an organized individual who can deal quickly and effectively with problems that may cause a change in production plans. Producers need to have a good sense of what stories, news, or other items will interest viewers. They also need salesmanship qualities since they may have to "sell" a station on a project idea or convince an actor to take a role. Producers work with teams of professionals and must be able to bring people together to work on the single goal of completing a project.

While working in the television world may seem glamorous, you should realize that as a producer your work will take place behind the scenes. Although people recognize stars of sitcoms and news anchors when they are in public, few are able to spot a producer in a crowd. You must be self-confident and be comfortable with anonymity if you are to enjoy this work.

EXPLORING

Consider joining the staff of your high school newspaper. This will give you experience in completing projects on a deadline, and, if you

Did You Know?

- Approximately 110,200,000 households in the United States subscribe to cable television.
- 28.5 million households subscribe to digital cable.
- The average U.S. household watches television for an average of eight hours and 11 minutes per day.

Source: National Cable & Telecommunications Association

are involved in selling ad space, you will get a taste of what it is like to work with budgets and financing. If your school has a radio or TV station, volunteer to be part of the staff. Become involved in the production work and you may learn how to use the cameras, control sound, or edit pieces. If your school doesn't have these facilities, consider joining the drama club. You will be able to do production work for a play and may also gain experience with advertising and financing the production.

To meet professionals in the field, ask your media department teacher or guidance counselor to arrange for a producer from a local TV station to come talk to interested students. Another option is to call the local TV station and request a tour of the facility. Explain that you are interested in becoming a producer and ask to meet a producer during your tour. You may also be able to set up an informational interview with the producer. Come to this interview prepared to ask questions. What type of educational background does this producer have? What is the hardest part of the job? What is the most enjoyable part? Does the producer have any advice for you? People are often happy to talk about their work when you have specific questions to ask and show a true interest. You may even find that you can develop a mentor relationship through this contact.

EMPLOYERS

Producers may be salaried employees of television stations or networks, or they may work independently, running their own production companies. Independent producers may take on projects for networks as well as other organizations. Producers who work on newscasts are employed across the country at large as well as medium-sized and small stations. Producers who work on television series typically live in Los Angeles, where many network headquarters are located. However, some producers live in New York City.

STARTING OUT

The job of producer is not an entry-level position. You will need to "pay your dues" by gaining experience working with different equipment and people. Internships are often the best way to break into the business. Interns are frequently offered paid positions after they graduate from school. If your internship doesn't lead to employment, make yourself visible in the field and take any job that allows you to work as a member of the production team.

Freddy James got his first job his junior year of college after a tour of a TV station. "I made sure the executive producer knew who I was when I left that day," he says. While most of the other students were interested in anchoring, James stressed his interest in producing. "And I sent a follow-up letter to the executive producer. The next thing I knew, they called wanting to know if I wanted to run a studio camera for minimum wage." The station was number one in the city, and James took the job knowing it would be an excellent opportunity to get a start in the field.

ADVANCEMENT

Advancement for producers depends to an extent on their individual goals. They may change stations, moving from smaller stations to larger ones where they oversee a larger staff and have increased pay. Some producers may decide to specialize, working in an area that interests them such as live broadcasts or music videos. Most consider it an advancement to work on their own projects. At some stations, an executive producer will oversee the work of one or more producers. Independent producers may advance by increasing their clientele and working on large-budget projects.

EARNINGS

Although producers who work for their own production companies or for the larger television networks can make well over $200,000 a year, most producers make considerably less. Bringing in the big paychecks as a producer for television comes from years of hard work, good luck, and well-established connections. But good producers don't generally enter the field with big money in mind—they love the work. Producers who don't make a great deal of money benefit in other ways: They often call all the shots and have control of a project.

According to the U.S. Department of Labor, producers and directors earned salaries that ranged from less than $26,940 to more than $84,190 in 2004. Producers and directors employed in radio and television broadcasting earned mean annual salaries of $55,400.

Producers who are full-time, salaried employees of stations or networks typically receive benefits such as health insurance and paid vacation and sick days. Independent producers must provide these extras for themselves.

WORK ENVIRONMENT

TV stations are generally clean, comfortable places equipped with up-to-date, sophisticated broadcasting equipment. The atmosphere is busy and exciting, with numerous professionals concentrating on completing their specific jobs. Some producers, such as Freddy James, may need to travel and work on location. The conditions for those working on location vary. For example, the producer may have to stand in the rain for hours with the crew attempting to get the right shot.

Creator and co–executive producer Anthony Zucker discusses a scene with stars of the television series *CSI: Crime Scene Investigation. (Landov)*

The work of a producer is stressful, both for those who work on live programming and those who work on taped programming. The producer needs to be a creative and fast-acting problem solver because production difficulties arise almost every day. A lot of people are needed to put on a television show, and personalities sometimes clash, which can lead to tension on the set. The producer must be able to work successfully in this atmosphere.

A producer's schedule will depend on the projects he or she is working on. A producer of a morning news show, for example, may need to be at the station by 4 A.M. A producer working on a television movie, on the other hand, might not need to be at the shoot until midday but work until late in the night. No matter what the project, though, long workdays (10 to 12 hours) are common.

OUTLOOK

According to the U.S. Department of Labor, the employment of actors, directors, and producers is expected to increase at an average rate through 2014, with many people trying to break into television production. New cable networks needing original programming are developing at a rapid rate. Freelance opportunities are also expected to increase as networks look to independent production companies for more programming. Producers will also be in demand to put together newscasts: newsrooms provide TV stations with healthy profits every year. Because many consider this exciting and glamorous work, however, competition for jobs will be high. TV producers (and those just starting out in the business) who have a thorough knowledge of new technologies will be in the best position to get jobs. Producers will not only need to understand various computer-assisted techniques, but, as broadcasting becomes more closely involved with the Internet and interactive television, producers will also need to know how to work with these technologies.

FOR MORE INFORMATION

For more information on the industry and training programs, contact
Directors Guild of America
7920 Sunset Boulevard
Los Angeles, CA 90046-3304
Tel: 310-289-2000
http://www.dga.org

For information on summer internships, contact
Institute of Political Journalism
The Fund for American Studies
1706 New Hampshire Avenue, NW
Washington, DC 20009-2502
Tel: 800-741-6964
http://www.dcinternships.org/ipj

For more industry news and career information, contact
Producers Guild of America
8530 Wilshire Boulevard, Suite 450
Beverly Hills, CA 90211-3115
Tel: 310-358-9020
Email: info@producersguild.org
http://www.producersguild.org

*RTNDA, an organization for electronic media news professionals, has
information on internships, scholarships, and the news industry.*
Radio-Television News Directors Association (RTNDA)
1600 K Street, NW, Suite 700
Washington, DC 20006-2838
Tel: 202-659-6510
Email: rtnda@rtnda.org
http://www.rtnda.org

To read television news online, check out the following Web site:
The Hollywood Reporter.com
http://www.hollywoodreporter.com

Weather Forecasters

OVERVIEW

Weather forecasters compile and analyze weather information and prepare reports for daily and nightly TV or radio newscasts. Forecasters, also known as *meteorologists* and *weathercasters*, create graphics, write scripts, and explain weather maps to audiences. They also provide special reports during extreme weather conditions. To predict future weather patterns and to develop increased accuracy in weather study and forecasting, forecasters may conduct research on such subjects as atmospheric electricity, clouds, precipitation, hurricanes, and data collected from weather satellites. Other areas of research used to forecast weather may include ocean currents and temperature.

HISTORY

Meteorology—the science that deals with the atmosphere and weather—is an observational science, involving the study of such factors as air pressure, climate, and wind velocity. Basic weather instruments were invented hundreds of years ago. Galileo invented the thermometer in 1593, and Evangelista Torricelli invented the barometer in 1643. Simultaneous comparison and study of weather in different areas was impossible until the telegraph was invented. Observations of the upper atmosphere from balloons and airplanes started after World War I. Not until World War II, however, was great financial support given to the development of meteorology. During this war, a very clear-cut relationship was established between the effectiveness of new weapons and the atmosphere.

More accurate instruments for measuring and observing weather conditions, new systems of communication, and the development of satellites, radar, and high-speed computers to process and analyze weather data have helped weather forecasters and the general public get a better understanding of the atmosphere.

THE JOB

El Niño. F5-rated tornadoes storming down tornado alley. Heat waves and ice storms. Fires started by floods in North Dakota. Hurricanes Andrew, Hugo, Betsy, and Katrina. Extreme weather conditions often become national celebrities while the citizens of the threatened cities suffer. These people look to TV and radio weather forecasters to advise them of upcoming storms, how to prepare for them, and how to recover from them. But weather forecasters aren't just on the air during extreme conditions—they're on radio and TV broadcasts many times every day. On one day, people may rely on their local forecaster to help them prepare for a midnight tornado; on another day, they may simply want to know whether to leave the house with an umbrella.

Some weather forecasters are reporters with broadcasting degrees, but approximately half of TV and radio weather forecasters have degrees in meteorology. Colleges across the country offer courses and degrees in meteorology for people who want to work for broadcast stations, weather services, research centers, flight centers, universities, and other places that study and record the weather. With a good background in the atmospheric sciences, broadcast weather forecasters can make informed predictions about the weather and can clearly explain these predictions to the public. The people of Myrtle Beach, South Carolina, look to Ed Piotrowski of WPDE-TV for the daily weather news as well as information on extreme weather conditions such as approaching hurricanes. As chief meteorologist for WPDE, Piotrowski is responsible for delivering the forecast for radio and three television evening newscasts. "I also manage a staff and several interns," he notes.

Preparing the forecast means interpreting a great deal of data from a variety of different sources. The data comes from weather stations, sometimes from different places around the world. Even the weather conditions swirling over the oceans can affect the weather of states far inland, so local weather forecasters keep track of the weather affecting distant cities. In addition, weather stations and ships at sea record atmospheric measurements, information that is then transmitted to other weather stations for analysis. This information makes its way to the National Weather Service in Washington, D.C., where scientists develop predictions to send to regional centers across the country. The tools used by meteorologists include weather balloons, instrumented aircraft, radar, satellites, and computers. Instrumented aircraft are high-performance airplanes used to observe many kinds of weather. Radar is used to detect rain or snow as well as other weather. Doppler radar can measure wind speed and direction. It has become the best tool for predicting severe weather. Satellites use advanced remote sensing to measure temperature, wind, and other characteristics of the atmosphere at many levels. Scientists can observe the entire surface of the earth with satellites. The introduction of computers has forever changed the research and forecasting of weather. The fastest computers are used in atmospheric research and for large-scale weather forecasting. Computers are used to produce simulations of upcoming weather.

At Piotrowski's station, the weather center receives information from the National Center for Environmental Prediction, the Storm Prediction Center (formerly known as the Severe Storms Forecast Center), the local National Weather Service offices, and the National Hurricane Center. Data also comes in from many different cities around the world. He explains, "All the data collected is put into many computer programs with various scientific formulas. These programs eventually put out weather scenarios for several different times in the future. Our job is to interpret these and make our forecast accordingly."

Though Piotrowski relies on his education and background in meteorology to work with the various tools of the weather center, he points out that weather computers vary in their operation. "Most of this is learned on the job," he says. And the technology is rapidly changing. "Doppler radar is constantly evolving. The computers are getting fancier and faster."

Broadcast weather forecasters may also prepare maps and graphics to aid their viewers. Broadcasting the information means reading and explaining the weather forecast to viewers and listeners. The broadcast weather forecaster must be able to concentrate on several different tasks at once. For example, when Piotrowski broadcasts to the TV audience, he is actually standing in front of a plain blue wall (called a chromakey) that shows graphics only to the viewers. In order for Piotrowski to see the map, he must watch the station's monitor. He then points to areas on the blue wall based on what he sees in the monitor; to the audience, it looks as though he is pointing to places on the map. While talking about the forecast, Piotrowski may have to listen to time cues (the amount of time left for the presentation) from the newscast producer through a hearing device placed in his ear. Throughout all this activity, the broadcast weather forecaster must stay focused and calm.

Many people look to TV and radio news for weather information to help them plan events and vacations. Farmers are often able to protect their crops by following weather forecasts and advisories. The weather forecast is a staple element of most TV and radio newscasts. Some cable and radio stations broadcast weather reports 24 hours a day; most local network affiliates broadcast reports during morning, noon, and evening newscasts, as well as provide extended weather coverage during storms and other extreme conditions. Piotrowski realizes that his responsibilities are vitally important during hurricanes. He explains, "We need to interpret the data to give people the scenario we think will play out in our area upon landfall. It could be the difference between life and death."

In addition to broadcasting weather reports, radio and TV weather forecasters often visit schools and community centers to speak on weather safety. They are also frequently involved in broadcast station promotions, taking part in community events.

REQUIREMENTS

High School
While you are in high school, you can prepare for a career as a broadcast weather forecaster by taking a number of different classes. Concentrate on the sciences—earth science, biology, chemistry, and physics—to develop an understanding of the environment and how different elements interact. Geography and mathematics courses will also be useful to you. To familiarize yourself with computers and gain experience working with graphics programs, take computer classes. Computers are an essential tool that you'll use throughout your career. Take plenty of English and speech classes. As a broadcaster, you will need to have excellent writing and speaking skills. If your school offers any media courses in which you learn how to broadcast a radio or television show, be sure to take such classes.

Postsecondary Training
Although a degree in meteorology or atmospheric science isn't required to enter the profession, it is necessary for advancement. The American Meteorological Society (AMS) offers a listing of schools, with extensive information about each program, at its Web site, http://www.ametsoc.org/amsucar_curricula/index.cfm. More than

100 programs are listed at the AMS Web site; these programs offer such courses as atmospheric measurements, thermodynamics and chemistry, radar, cloud dynamics, and physical climatology.

While in college, you should also continue to take English, speech, and communications classes to hone your communication skills and computer classes to keep up to date with this technology. It is also important during your college years to complete an internship as a student weather forecaster with a TV or radio station. Your college and organizations such as the AMS can help you locate an internship. Although it may not pay much—if anything—this position will allow you to make contacts with professionals and give you hands-on experience.

Certification or Licensing
The American Meteorological Society offers three certification programs: the certified broadcast meteorologist program, the seal of approval, and the certified consulting meteorologist program. In addition, the National Weather Association (NWA) also offers a seal of approval to broadcast meteorologists. Contact the AMS and NWA for information on eligibility requirements. Certification isn't required for broadcast weather forecasters to work in the business, but it will give you an edge when looking for a job.

Other Requirements
As a broadcast weather forecaster, you must be able to work well under pressure in order to meet deadlines for programming or plot severe weather systems. You must be able to communicate complex theories and events in a manner that is easy for your audience to

Deadliest U.S. Hurricanes

Hurricane Name	Year	Category*	# of Deaths
1. Galveston, Tex.	1900	4	8,000
2. Lake Okeechobee, Fla.	1928	4	1,836
3. Katrina (La./Miss.)	2005	4	1,200
4. Florida Keys/S. Tex.	1919	4	600
5. New England	1938	5	600

Source: National Oceanic and Atmospheric Administration
* based on a scale of 1 to 5, with 5 being the most devastating

understand. And, naturally, you must have an interest in weather and the environment. "Don't go into TV weather just to be on TV," Ed Piotrowski advises. "You must have a passion for the weather to do a fantastic job."

EXPLORING

There are several ways you can explore different aspects of this career while you are still in school. Consider joining a science club involved in environmental activities. Ask a teacher or guidance counselor to schedule a trip to a local television station so you can see firsthand what this work environment is like. It is also a good idea to volunteer to work at your school's radio or TV station. You'll learn the basics of putting on a program and might even get on the air yourself. If your school doesn't have one of these stations, join the newspaper staff to get some experience working with the media. In addition, pay attention to the weathercasters on your local news and on The Weather Channel (http://www.weatherchannel.com) to become familiar with how to deliver your forecasts.

Each year, the National Weather Service (NWS) accepts a limited number of student volunteers, mostly college students but also a few high school students. Local offices of the NWS also allow the public to come in for tours by appointment. Your guidance counselor may be able to help you with this.

Also, contact your local radio and TV stations and ask for a tour. Tell them you are interested in broadcast meteorology and ask to meet the weather forecasting staff. You may be able to arrange for an informational interview with the weather forecaster, during which you might ask that person about his or her education, experiences, the best part of the work, and any other questions you may have.

EMPLOYERS

Most broadcast weather forecasters work for network television affiliates and local radio stations. Because evening national newscasts do not have weather forecasts, there are fewer network opportunities for broadcast meteorologists. National cable networks, such as The Weather Channel and 24-hour news channels, hire weather forecasters and may offer internships.

Those who have degrees in meteorology or atmospheric science can work for a variety of other services as well—the United States government is the largest employer of meteorologists in the country. Meteorologists work for the NWS, the military, the Department of Agriculture, and other agencies.

STARTING OUT

Your college's career services office is a good resource to use when you are looking for your first job. Many people also find their first positions either through connections they have made while interning or through the internship itself. Ed Piotrowski's first full-time job was with the TV station where he interned. "I was very fortunate," he says. "I showed great initiative and the weekend job opened up right around the time I graduated."

Local ads and job listings on the Internet are other sources you should check out. The AMS and the NWA send members job listings and also post openings on their Web sites.

ADVANCEMENT

Someone forecasting for a network affiliate in a smaller region may want to move to a larger city and a larger audience. In many cases, though, meteorologists work their way up within one station. Full-time broadcast meteorologists generally start forecasting for the weekend news or the morning news and then move up to the evening news. A meteorologist may then become *chief meteorologist,* in charge of a newscast's weather center and staff.

EARNINGS

In the newsroom, weather forecasters generally make more than sportscasters but less than lead anchors. The salary for weather forecasters varies greatly according to experience, region, and media. Those working in television typically earn more than those working in radio. According to the U.S. Department of Labor, the median annual income for announcers in radio and television broadcasting was $22,820 in 2004. Weather forecasters with degrees in meteorology stand to earn more money. Atmospheric scientists (an occupational group that includes meteorologists) earned salaries ranging from less than $35,480 to more than $107,690. Those employed in radio and television broadcasting had mean annual earnings of $77,250 in 2004. Weather forecasters working in stations that serve large metropolitan areas such as New York and Houston may make more money than their colleagues in smaller markets.

WORK ENVIRONMENT

The atmosphere at a radio or TV station can be exciting, fun, and sometimes tense—especially during times of emergency. Forecasters' schedules depend on the times they are scheduled to be on the air. Those working morning shows, for example, may have to be at the station by 4:00 A.M. to prepare for the broadcast. The weather forecaster may also make public appearances, giving talks to schools or clubs. This gives the forecaster the opportunity to meet a lot of people and attend events; however, it also makes for busy and varied days. In addition, they have to be prepared to work odd or long hours during times of weather emergencies.

Weather forecasters work with a great deal of specialized equipment, such as computers and radar, as well as the equipment of the broadcast trade, such as the chromakey, hearing devices, and microphones. The weather forecaster is part of a team (along with such professionals as newscasters, producers, and technicians) who work to put the broadcast on the air.

OUTLOOK

The U.S. Department of Labor predicts that employment for all atmospheric scientists will increase about as fast as the average through 2014. However, the Labor Department also predicts that employment for television and radio announcers will decline throughout the same time period. Usually, meteorologists are able to find work in the field upon graduation, though they may have to be flexible about the area of meteorology and region of the country in which they work. Positions for broadcast meteorologists, as with any positions in broadcast news, are in high demand. The number of news departments and news staffs is expected to increase at a steady rate, but the growing number of graduates looking for work in news departments will keep the field very competitive.

Currently, about half of TV and radio weather forecasters do not hold meteorology degrees; with increased competition for work, forecasters without extensive backgrounds in the atmospheric sciences may find it difficult to get jobs. New tools and computer programs for the compilation and analyses of data are constantly being developed by research scientists. To find good positions, future broadcast meteorologists will need a lot of technical expertise in addition to their understanding of weather.

A national fascination with weather may lead to more outlets for broadcast meteorologists. Weather disasters are requiring more coverage by news departments. In addition to forecasting, broadcast meteorologists will be involved in reporting the after-effects of storms and other extreme conditions. Many people look to the Internet for global and regional weather information, so look for broadcast and Internet weather resources to merge. Broadcast meteorologists are becoming more actively involved in developing and maintaining pages on the Internet.

FOR MORE INFORMATION

This organization has information on meteorology careers, student membership, and education. For more information, contact
American Meteorological Society
45 Beacon Street
Boston, MA 02108-3693
Tel: 617-227-2425
Email: amsinfo@ametsoc.org
http://www.ametsoc.org/AMS

For weather and employment information and links to other weather-related sites, check out the following Web site:
National Oceanic and Atmospheric Administration
14th Street and Constitution Avenue, NW, Room 6217
Washington, DC 20230-0001
Tel: 202-482-6090
Email: answers@noaa.gov
http://www.noaa.gov

To read selected sections of the monthly NWA Newsletter or find out about local chapters, check out the following Web site:
National Weather Association (NWA)
1697 Capri Way
Charlottesville, VA 22911-3534
Tel: 434-296-9966
Email: NatWeaAsoc@aol.com
http://www.nwas.org

To learn more about the weather, take a look at the NWS's Web site:
National Weather Service (NWS)
1325 East-West Highway
Silver Spring, MD 20910-3280
Tel: 301-713-0258
http://www.nws.noaa.gov

This Web site, presented by the University of Illinois, provides an overview of meteorology for high school and undergraduate students:
WW2010
http://ww2010.atmos.uiuc.edu

Index